Harold Lubell

Urban development and employment: the prospects for Calcutta

Foreword by J. Tinbergen

International Labour Office Geneva

309.262
L

ISBN (paperback) 92-2-101085-6
      (hardback)   92-2-101091-0

First published 1974

PRINTED BY KLAUSFELDER, VEVEY, SWITZERLAND

FOREWORD

Even those who have had only superficial impressions of the city of Calcutta and its surroundings have been struck by the immense human problems in that area. They are problems that have grown out of a cumulation of events and for which the local authorities and the Governments of West Bengal and India cannot be reasonably held solely responsible. The main developments are quite well known. In 1912 the seat of the Government of India was moved from Calcutta to Delhi. In 1947 the partition of independent India brought large numbers of refugees from East Pakistan. Like all large cities in developing countries, Calcutta has been a centre of attraction for the surplus population of the surrounding countryside. The influx of jobless persons exceeded the absorptive capacity of the labour market and created extremely acute housing problems. The expansion of employment opportunities was relatively satisfactory in the 1950s and early 1960s; but a new series of unfavourable events—a slump and two years of bad crops—caused a further deterioration of conditions in the area. Even though a broadly based and effective start had been made, with the support of the Ford Foundation, on a 20-year development plan for the Metropolitan District of Calcutta, the governments at the various levels concerned found it virtually impossible to put the plan fully into practice.

In recent years, however, a series of positive events have fortunately occurred and hopes have revived that the co-operation of various agencies involved, each of them benefiting from a considerable stock of local talent, will turn the tide. Among these new events, it is the internal ones that are the most important: Mrs. Gandhi's party received strong support; the events leading to the creation of Bangladesh gave added self-confidence to the local and regional authorities; an important new source of inspiration on the best way to tackle the problem of development has come from the new State Planning Board of the Government of West Bengal. Thanks to that Board, a new strategy for development, in the elaboration of which Dr. A. N. Bose played a leading part, was formulated on the basis of an integrated development of both the rural surroundings and the city so that development of the one will reinforce development of the other.

The ILO rightly saw in Calcutta one of the most promising areas in which to initiate a co-operative research effort at the international level under the World Employment Programme. Harold Lubell, who probably knows better than any non-Indian student of the area its complicated structure, its history and the feasibility of the components of the new integrated strategy, sets out, in this volume of the World Employment Programme series of research publications, the many aspects of this complex proposed activity and its multifarious background. With the full co-operation of the authorities and persons involved, he provides the reader interested in development problems with a systematic and careful account of his subject, based on well selected source material.

Now that the first review and appraisal of the Second Development Decade has been carried out by the United Nations Development Planning Committee, this study provides an outstanding example of what can be undertaken in international co-operation in one of the parts of the world that are most in need of such co-operation. I hope it will be an eye-opener to many responsible politicians and their advisers. A forceful response to Mr. Lubell's study will be the best reward for the author and for those responsible, both nationally and internationally, for the implementation of the World Employment Programme.

J. TINBERGEN

CONTENTS

Conventional signs and designations:

.   Not available

— Nil or negligible

Rs 1 crore = Rs 100 lakhs = Rs 10,000,000

PREFACE

The World Employment Programme is the main ILO contribution to the International Development Strategy for the Second United Nations Development Decade. The aims of the Programme are to identify particular policies and measures to improve the employment situation in the developing countries and to assist in the implementation of such policies and measures. Four principal means of action have been developed under the Programme—comprehensive exploratory country employment missions, regional employment teams for Africa, Asia, and Latin America and the Caribbean, country employment teams, and an action-oriented research programme.

In the research carried out under the Programme, particular stress is laid on the undertaking of country-based case studies with the co-operation of local research institutions, government agencies and individuals; the aim is to put forward practical suggestions based on the increased knowledge resulting from the studies. The research programme at present includes seven major projects, dealing respectively with technology and employment, income distribution and employment, population and employment, education and employment, urbanisation and employment, trade expansion and employment, and emergency employment schemes. The present monograph is a product of the urbanisation and employment project[1], and is the report on the first of a series of city case studies that are being financed primarily by a grant from the Government of the Federal Republic of Germany.

The author[2] is indebted to a number of people in Calcutta and in New Delhi who provided help, ideas, information and advice at an early stage of

[1] The first publication issued under the urbanisation and employment project was originally prepared as a background paper. See Paul Bairoch: *Urban unemployment in developing countries: The nature of the problem and proposals for its solution* (Geneva, ILO, 1973).

[2] Harold Lubell is project manager of the urbanisation and employment research project under the ILO World Employment Programme, and has had many years of experience as a development economist with the United Nations, the Rand Corporation, the Ford Foundation, the United States Agency for International Development and other organisations.

the preparation of this report; they include H. Banerji, B. N. Bhattacharya, Sudhir Bhattacharyya, I. Z. Bhatty, S. Bhootalingam, Ajit N. Bose, C. S. Chandrasekhara, B. K. Chatterjee, Bhaskar Ghose, P. C. Khanna, Chitta Mitra, Swapan K. Mookerjee, Moni Mukherjee, Sudhendu Mukherjee, S. Naqvi, Tapan Piplai, P. Prabakhar Rao, Arthur Row, K. C. Sivaramakrishnan, S. V. Sethuraman and R. D. Vidyarthi.

A first draft of the study was submitted to a meeting on Calcutta's employment problem which was held at the International Labour Office in Geneva in February 1973 and was attended by Paul Bairoch, I. Z. Bhatty, Ajit N. Bose, Edgar O. Edwards, J. Tinbergen and John Weeks. The present version has been revised in the light of their comments, as well as of criticism and suggestions by Louis Emmerij, Shyam R. Gupta, Angus Hone and James M. Pines. However, responsibility for any errors of fact or conception that may remain lies with the author alone.

The cut-off date for data used in this report was March 1973.

INTRODUCTION

At the end of the first decade of the eighteenth century, the future city of Calcutta was a small settlement of some 10,000 inhabitants.[1] Today, there are some 7 million persons dwelling in Greater Calcutta, now India's largest urban agglomeration.[2]

It was in the 1680s that an English enterprise, the East India Company, chose as the site of a local centre for its trading with eastern India a cluster of neighbouring hamlets located 120 miles inland from the Bay of Bengal on the left bank of the River Hooghly, which was at that time[3] the main channel of the Ganges on its way to the sea. By the middle of the eighteenth century, a city of some 200,000 inhabitants had been built on that site, and by 1850 the size of Calcutta's population had grown to about 400,000.

A first systematic enumeration of the population of India carried out in 1872 gave a figure of 633,000 as the number of inhabitants in the city of Calcutta. It was not yet, however, India's most populated city: on the other side of the Indian sub-continent, Bombay, which had 10,000 inhabitants towards the end of the seventeenth century, had increased its population to 644,000 in 1872.

Four decades later, the 1911 Census showed that the populations of the Municipal Corporations of Calcutta and of Greater Bombay had drawn level at about one million inhabitants each. This was twice the size of the population of the next two largest cities of India—Madras and Hyderabad.[4]

---

[1] All population figures given in the present chapter for the seventeenth, eighteenth and nineteenth centuries are taken from E. A. Gait's chapter on "Population" in *The Imperial Gazetteer of India* (Oxford, Clarendon Press, 1909), Vol. I.

[2] See below, table 1, p. 35.

[3] See below, Annex B, p. 114.

[4] *Census of India, 1961,* Paper No. 1 of 1967: *Working force 1901/1961* (New Delhi, 1968), subsidiary table B-II.3 (i), pp. 41, 61, 67, 96.

In the meantime, a vast conurbation extending both northwards and southwards, as well as westwards to the right bank of the Hooghly River, had begun to build up around the old city of Calcutta. By the time of the 1971 Census, the population of this Greater Calcutta had expanded, as already mentioned, to 7 million, while that of Greater Bombay had grown to only 6 million.[1] As for the city of Calcutta itself, its population had increased to 3.1 million.[2]

It was as the major British trading centre for eastern India and, moreover, as the political capital of India until 1912[3] that Calcutta had originally attracted to it all the modern urban activities—export and import trade, finance, political administration and industry. Calcutta is still the major urban centre of a vast region including rural West Bengal, Bihar to the north-west, Orissa to the south-west, Assam and the neighbouring hill states to the north-east and the eastern states beyond present-day Bangladesh.

A significant peculiarity of Calcutta's regional location is that, unlike Delhi and even Bombay, Calcutta has no other major urban centre within hundreds of miles of it in India. The other cities in the Eastern Region of India[4] outside of Calcutta are all provincial centres with small populations and limited ranges of economic activities and employment opportunities. Moreover, Bangladesh, as East Pakistan, was cut off from normal contact with West Bengal and Calcutta from 1947 to 1971.

The development of India's coal and steel industries at some distance to the west of Calcutta at Asansol-Durgapur, Bokaro, Ranchi, Jamshedpur and Rourkela has undoubtedly created other possible urban growth points, but on a so much smaller scale that they can hardly counter the overwhelming attraction of Calcutta within the Eastern Region. Nevertheless, the future development of the so-called South East Resource Region[5] does offer some promise of other centres of mining, industrial and urban growth within the field of attraction of Calcutta.

---

[1] United Nations: *Demographic yearbook, 1971—23rd Issue*; *Special topic: Population census statistics I* (New York, 1972), table 9, p. 361.

[2] *Census of India, 1971*, Series 18: *West Bengal*, Paper 1 of 1971: *Provisional population totals*, by Bashkar Ghose, Director of Census Operations, West Bengal (Calcutta, 1971), table I, p. 49.

[3] In 1912, the seat of the Government of India was transferred from Calcutta to Delhi.

[4] See map 3.

[5] See Government of India, Ministry of Works, Housing and Urban Development, Town and Country Planning Organisation, Joint Planning Board for South East Resource Region: *Regional development plan for South East Resource Region: Summary report* [New Delhi, 1972], mimeographed. The South East Resource Region comprises parts of the states of Madhya Pradesh, Orissa, Bihar and West Bengal; it is centred on the Mahanadi River basin. The existing industrial areas within it comprise the Bhilai-Durg area about 50 km west of Raipur and the areas of Jamshedpur, Ranchi and the upper Damodar Valley in the east (including, in West Bengal, the Purulia and Bankura Districts and the Asansol and Durgapur subdivisions of the Burdwan District).

Calcutta's importance as an economic centre for all of India stems from the concentration of industry, financial services and trade activities within the city and in the Calcutta Metropolitan District.[1] All of these grew out of the concentration of British trading and, later, industrial activity in Bengal from the days of the East India Company. Consequently, an enormous amount of privately generated capital was, over the past century, accumulated in metropolitan Calcutta. In view of the limited resources available at state and national levels, it makes sense to build on this existing capital stock rather than to fritter it away or abandon it by permitting Calcutta to continue to decline.

The main industrial activities of metropolitan Calcutta are jute processing and metal-working (engineering). The jute mills extend above and below the city of Calcutta on both banks of the Hooghly River. The engineering industries are concentrated at Calcutta on the east bank and at Howrah on the west bank opposite the city. In 1966/67, West Bengal accounted for 21.6 per cent of India's export earnings through exports of jute manufactures alone; but in 1970/71 the share of jute manufactures had fallen to 12.4 per cent.[2] As the major centre for heavy engineering despite the recent spread of industrialisation to other areas, metropolitan Calcutta and the Asansol-Durgapur steel producing area of West Bengal have been the largest Indian suppliers of investment goods under the Five-Year Plans and, until the late 1960s, of engineering goods for export.

As the main port for the Gangetic Plain and for India's Eastern Region, Calcutta handled in its peak year (1966/67) around a fifth of the total volume of the cargo moving in India's foreign trade: 17 per cent of imports and 30 per cent of exports.[3] The exports consisted primarily of commodities derived from two agricultural industries established close to Calcutta: jute products from West Bengal and tea from the mountains of northern West

---

[1] The Calcutta Metropolitan District (CMD), also referred to in this study as "metropolitan Calcutta" or the "metropolis" of Calcutta, is a vast "conurbation formed around the cities and towns which have grown together in one linear and continuous pattern of urban development along both banks of the River Hooghly" (Government of West Bengal, Calcutta Metropolitan Planning Organisation: *Basic development plan for the Calcutta Metropolitan District, 1966-1986* (1966), p. 1). The CMD covers an area of 490 square miles (1,270 km²) and has a population of 8.3 million (1971 provisional estimate). It is not an administrative unit, local government being in the hands of Calcutta Corporation for the city of Calcutta itself and of a large number of other administrative units (municipal corporations, municipal towns, non-municipal towns and rural *mouzas*, or villages). For some particulars of the Calcutta Metropolitan Planning Organisation (CMPO), see below, Annex B. The Calcutta urban agglomeration (Greater Calcutta), as defined for census purposes, is smaller than the Calcutta Metropolitan District. The former comprises all the contiguous municipalities adjoining Calcutta and Howrah, while the latter also includes a number of rural areas on the fringes of Greater Calcutta, lying between certain non-contiguous municipalities.

[2] Government of India: *Economic survey, 1971-72* (New Delhi, Government of India Press, 1972), pp. 140-141.

[3] Government of India, Central Statistical Organisation: *Statistical abstract, India, 1969* (New Delhi, 1970), p. 343.

3

Bengal and Assam. In that year these two commodity groups accounted for 35 per cent of India's total export earnings, although by 1970/71 their share had fallen to only 22 per cent owing to an absolute decline in exports of both jute products and tea.[1]

One of Calcutta's most striking characteristics is its fantastic overcrowding. It is difficult for a casual visitor to grasp the physical significance of a population density figure of the order of 30,500 per square kilometre[2], since his initial visual impression of the city is of the open spaces of the Maidan[3] and the gardens along Chowringhee[4] and of the respectable facades of blocks of flats and offices put up in the city centre in the late nineteenth and early twentieth centuries. It is later that the visitor perceives an extraordinary difference between other big cities and Calcutta. Most of the world's large towns are laid out as the empty cells of a honeycomb with houses on the streets and empty spaces behind; in Calcutta's crowded districts, the cells behind the houses whose facade is on the street are almost completely covered with low structures. In some of the formerly more fashionable areas one will even find a decaying old eighteenth or nineteenth century town house still standing on its street front emplacement with a new block of flats of eight or ten storeys standing behind it in what used to be the back garden. One of the physical problems of town planning in Calcutta is consequently to divert growth to the periphery of the metropolis and to de-congest at least the main access routes to the centre.

Another peculiarity of Calcutta is the concentration within the city of persons with secondary and higher education and of institutions providing education to those levels. There are a number of reasons for Calcutta's high demand for secondary and higher education. One of them is that Calcutta has been a traditional centre of education since the nineteenth century "Bengali Renaissance"; indeed, Calcutta saw the opening of India's first English-language college, Hindu College, in 1817 and of the University of Calcutta in 1857. Another reason is the concentration in Calcutta of higher caste Bengali Hindus, who contributed much to learning and scholarship. In earlier days, one of the consequences of British consolidation of the *zamindari* system[5] was gravitation of the landlords' families from the land to the big city, where they lived partly off agricultural rents and also took up white-collar jobs in the

---

[1] Government of India: *Economic survey, 1971-72*, op. cit., pp. 140-141.

[2] Provisional 1971 figure for the Census District of Calcutta.

[3] Area of about 1,000 acres on the land sides of Fort William, which stands on the east bank of the Hooghly near the centre of Calcutta; the area contains parade grounds, playing fields and some public buildings.

[4] Road running along the east side of the Maidan.

[5] A system of collection of revenues for the government from cultivators of land whereby the collector *(zamindar)* was subsequently given landowning rights.

British commercial and administrative system. Although the financial returns in such jobs were relatively attractive—and continue to be so—education also served as a mark of high social status.

In metropolitan Calcutta the rate of open unemployment is higher, and the waste of human resources is therefore perhaps greater, than in any other urban centre in India. The groups among which unemployment is heaviest also happen to be particularly active politically and probably account for a great deal of the political instability and violence for which Calcutta has been notorious. Even a partial solution to Calcutta's urban unemployment problem will contribute to the political and social stability of the metropolis and could demonstrate that even chronic social ills are amenable to gradual cure.

This monograph was written with a number of aims in view. One of them is to re-examine the anatomy of urban unemployment in one of India's great cities in the light of the general hypothesis[1] that urban unemployment in the developing countries is primarily a consequence of the fact that the increase in productive urban employment opportunities falls far short of the rapid increase in the urban labour force, the latter caused primarily by massive rural-urban migration. As the great Indian city with the highest apparent incidence of open unemployment, Calcutta is a good case for testing this hypothesis.

A second aim is to examine the extent to which a programme of urban infrastructure development can play a significant role in creating urban employment in a city where plans for major urban renewal and expansion exist and are likely to be implemented.

A third aim is to set out some other elements of an employment policy for urban employment creation specific to Calcutta, focusing particularly on the problem of unemployment of the educated Bengali middle class.

The general state of the economy as it has affected employment in West Bengal and Calcutta is discussed in Chapter 2. The body of existing information on migration, employment and unemployment in Calcutta is examined in Chapter 3. In Chapter 4, an attempt is made to consider the economic effect of development of Calcutta's infrastructure. Some of the other elements of a partial solution of Calcutta's employment problem are set out in Chapter 5. A summary of the study and some conclusions are given in a closing chapter.

---

[1] See Bairoch: *Urban unemployment in developing countries*, op. cit.

THE ECONOMIC SETTING

2

GROWTH AND STAGNATION IN THE 1960s

An over-all view

It was not until the mid-sixties that Calcutta's economy, which is primarily industrial, entered a phase of stagnation. During the period of the first three Five-Year Plans (1951-1965), net value added in manufacturing in West Bengal (large-scale and small-scale combined) rose, in constant prices, at the rather rapid average annual rate of 6.9 per cent[1]; employment in all registered factories rose at an average annual rate of 2.1 per cent[1], while employment in registered factories in the engineering sector rose at an average rate of 5.2 per cent per year.[2] In the latter part of that period (1959-1965), West Bengal's engineering industries recorded an average growth of 16.8 per cent per year in net value added at current prices (compared with 19.4 per cent per year for the rest of India) and of 8.3 per cent per year in employment.[3] This period of rapid expansion was, however, followed by a period of sharp recession.

The recession, which struck all India but was felt most acutely and for the longest time by West Bengal, and more particularly by metropolitan Calcutta, was the result of a combination of factors: foreign aid had been suspended during the Indo-Pakistan war of 1964 and there was a two-year succession of droughts which severely affected Indian agriculture and led the central Government to reduce its investment outlay in an attempt to hold back the drought-induced inflation. The area hardest hit by the reduction of government investment was West Bengal, which contains India's main concentration of engineering industries. Calcutta was particularly vulnerable to the cut-back in

---

[1] A. N. Bose: "Continuing semi-colonial character—The basic problem of the Indian metropolis", in *Indian Journal of Regional Science*, Vol. III, No. 1, 1971, p. 40.

[2] Calcutta Metropolitan Planning Organisation, Industrial Planning Team: *Report on the engineering industry, West Bengal, 1951-1968* (Calcutta, 1968), p. 6.

[3] Ibid., pp. 5, 9, 10.

government orders for engineering goods, which fell off sharply in 1965 when the targets of the Third Five-Year Plan were abandoned.

The rate of growth of Indian industrial production slowed down severely from 1966 onward. The all-India growth rate for value added in industry (broadly defined to include mining, manufacturing, construction, electricity) fell to an average of 3.6 per cent per year from 1965/66 to 1969/70.[1] Employment in manufacturing for all India fell by 1.9 per cent from 1966 to 1967 and then fell by a little more to 1968; a subsequent upturn to 1969 still left total employment below the 1966 level and it was not until 1970 that the annual figure showed some improvement (3.4 per cent) over 1966.[2]

In West Bengal, factory employment fell steadily from its 1966 peak of 880,000 to 791,000 in 1969, giving an average rate of decline of 2 per cent a year.[3] It did not rise again until 1970, when there was an upturn in the jute industry. The engineering industries, which had benefited most from the pre-1966 economic expansion, were the hardest hit after 1966; registered factory employment in the engineering sector in West Bengal fell at an average rate of 2.6 per cent per year from 1965 to 1969[4], and stagnated in 1970.

If, instead of declining during those years, employment in the engineering sector had continued to rise as in 1959-65 by 8 per cent per year, the social and political situation in Calcutta and in West Bengal as a whole might have been less troubled. The Bengalis who have entered the industrial labour force are especially heavily concentrated in the engineering (metal-working) industries[5], so that much of Calcutta's political troubles in recent years can probably be attributed to the increase in unemployment among Bengalis due to the stagnation in the engineering industries after 1965/66. Instead of being absorbed into industrial employment at an adequate rate, new members of the Bengali labour force found themselves surplus to already employed Bengalis who were being laid off. A major point of entry into a stable pattern of social living was thereby blocked.

Bengalis tend to attribute some of Calcutta's troubles also to a decision taken by T. T. Krishnamachari, India's Minister of Finance in the 1950s, to equalise prices of iron, steel, coal and cement throughout India, thereby depriving Calcutta of its locational advantage of proximity to the coal and iron centres in West Bengal and Bihar.

[1] Government of India: *Economic survey, 1971-72*, op. cit., pp. 75-76.

[2] End-of-March figures.

[3] A. N. Bose: "Continuing semi-colonial character", op. cit., p. 40; and Government of West Bengal: *Economic review, 1970-71*, p. 94.

[4] Calcutta Metropolitan Planning Organisation: *A note on the economic development programme for the Calcutta Metropolitan District*, A draft for discussion (1972, mimeographed), p. 9.

[5] See below, Chapter 3.

The intensity of Calcutta's economic setback during the post-1965 recession was due in part to some secondary effects of the general decline in industrial output which were peculiar to Calcutta—increased politicisation of Calcutta's economic life; disruption of production by politicised labour unions on "class struggle" grounds in factories otherwise unaffected by the recession; a much publicised breakdown of law and order; and the fact that the government of West Bengal came under the control of a coalition dominated by two Communist Parties. All these factors led to a shifting away from Calcutta of new private investment and probably also to a considerable flight of capital.

Value added and employment by sector

The structure of the Calcutta Metropolitan District's economy in the early 1960s is made clear in a set of estimates for 1961 on earners and net value added by sector; it was prepared by the Calcutta Metropolitan Planning Organisation (CMPO) and presented in a paper by H. Banerji[1] (see table 1). The estimates break down the economy into the standard three sectors: primary (agriculture and related activities), secondary (manufacturing and construction) and tertiary (trade, transport and other services). The extent of rural areas in the District being very limited, the primary sector accounted in 1961 for only 2.5 per cent of the total number of earners and for only 1.6 per cent of total value added. The secondary sector accounted for 41.3 per cent of earners and 56.8 per cent of net value added, with manufacturing alone accounting for, respectively, 38.4 per cent and 54.6 per cent. The tertiary sector occupied 56.2 per cent of earners and was the origin of 41.6 per cent of net value added. Estimated net value added per earner amounted to Rs 1,357 in the primary sector, Rs 2,917 in the secondary sector and Rs 1,567 in the tertiary sector.

Other estimates, relating to 1962, are given by A. N. Bose[2] (see table 2). They break down the District's economy into four sectors—primary; manufacturing; power, transport and construction; commerce and other services. Bose's two largest sectors are manufacturing and commerce, etc. The former accounted in 1962 for 39.0 per cent of total employment and 61.2 per cent of total gross income (gross value added) and the latter for, respectively, 45.6 per cent and 27.4 per cent.

---

[1] H. Banerji: *The socio-economic plan frame* (Calcutta Metropolitan Planning Organisation, 1966, mimeographed), p. 4.

[2] A. N. Bose: *Implications of capacity utilisation: A study of the Calcutta Metropolitan District* (Calcutta, Das Gupta, 1965), p. 10.

Table 1. Earners and net value added, Calcutta Metropolitan District, 1961

Sector and sub-sector	Earners ('000)	Net value added (Rs crores)[1]	Net value added per earner[2] (Rs)	Percentages	
				Earners	Net value added
Primary	58.6	8.0	1 357	2.5	1.6
Secondary	964.6	281.4	2 917	41.3	56.8
Manufacturing	897.4	270.6	3 015	38.4	54.6
Large	519.6	176.8	3 403	22.2	36.0
Medium large	35.9	15.7	4 369	1.5	3.2
Medium	33.5	14.8	4 424	1.4	3.0
Small	308.4	63.3	2 052	13.2	12.8
Construction	67.2	10.7	1 603	2.9	2.2
Tertiary	1 314.3	206.0	1 567	56.2	41.6
Transport, communications	228.4	44.1	1 930	9.8	8.9
Railways	82.8	22.8	2 749	3.5	4.6
Other	145.6	21.3	1 465	6.2	4.3
Trade, commerce	450.1	85.7	1 903	19.2	17.3
Banking, insurance	10.7	5.7	5 319	0.4	1.2
Big trade	106.9	29.6	2 772	4.6	6.0
Small trade	332.5	50.3	1 514	14.2	10.2
Services, professions	635.8	76.2	1 199	27.2	15.4
Domestic service	290.4	14.8	511	12.4	3.0
Professions, liberal arts	220.4	41.7	1 892	9.4	8.4
Public services	125.0	19.7	1 576	5.3	4.0
Total	2 337.5	495.3	2 120	100.0	100.0

[1] Rs 1 crore = Rs 100 lakhs = Rs 10 million.   [2] Calculated in the source from figures in Rs lakhs.

Source: H. Banerji: *The socio-economic plan frame* (Calcutta Metropolitan Planning Organisation, 1966, mimeographed), p. 4.

Table 2. Estimated gross value added and employment, by sector, Calcutta Metropolitan District, 1962

Sector	Gross value added (Rs crores) (1)	Total employment ('000) (2)	Income per employee (1) ÷ (2) (Rs) (3)	Percentages	
				Gross value added (4)	Total employment (5)
Primary	8.0	60	1 333	1.4	2.5
Manufacturing	361.1	926	3 900	61.2	39.0
Power, transport, construction	59.0	307	1 922	10.0	12.9
Commerce and other services	162.0	1 086	1 488	27.4	45.6
Total	590.1	2 379	2 477	100.0	100.0

Source: A. N. Bose: *Implications of capacity utilisation: A study of the Calcutta Metropolitan District* (Calcutta, Das Gupta, 1965), p. 10.

Table 3. Working population by broad sector, Calcutta Metropolitan District and West Bengal, 1961

Sector	Absolute numbers (in thousands)			Percentages			CMD¹ as % of W. Bengal
	CMD¹	Rest of W. Bengal	Total W. Bengal	CMD¹	Rest of W. Bengal	Total W. Bengal	
Agriculture and related activities	40	6 190	6 230	1.7	67.2	53.8	0.6
Mining and manufacturing	930	1 452	2 382	39.3	15.8	20.6	39.0
Transport and construction	299	247	546	12.6	2.6	4.7	54.8
Trade and services	1 097	1 325	2 422	46.4	14.4	20.9	45.3
Total	2 366	9 214	11 580	100.0	100.0	100.0	20.4

¹ Calcutta Metropolitan District.

Source: A. N. Bose: *Implications of capacity utilisation,* op. cit., p. 8, quoting 1961 Census of India.

Table 4. Estimated net value added by sector, Calcutta Metropolitan District (1961) and West Bengal (1960/61)

Sector	Rs crores		Percentages	
	Metro-politan Calcutta 1961 (1)	West Bengal 1960/61 (2)	Metro-politan Calcutta 1961 (3)	West Bengal 1960/61 (4)
Agriculture and related activities	8.0	414.3	1.6	38.0
Mining	—	27.3	—	2.5
Manufacturing	270.6	234.2	54.6	21.5
Large	(176.8)	(175.3)	(35.7)	(16.1)
Other	(93.8)	(58.9)	(18.9)	(5.4)
Construction	10.7	14.5	2.2	1.3
Transport, communication	44.1	62.4	8.9	5.7
Trade, commerce	85.7	98.5	17.3	9.0
Services, professions	76.2	239.4	15.4	22.0
Total net value added	495.3	1 090.7	100.0	100.0

Sources: col. (1): H. Banerji: *The socio-economic plan frame*, op. cit., p. 4; col. (2): Government of West Bengal: *Economic review, year 1971-72* (Calcutta, 1972), p. 68.

At the time of the 1961 Census of India[1], Calcutta accounted for 20 per cent of the total working force in West Bengal. The proportion in agriculture was less than 1 per cent, but it was 39 per cent in mining and manufacturing, 55 per cent in transport and communications and 45 per cent in trade and services (see table 3).

Neither the Banerji nor the Bose value-added figures for Calcutta can be directly compared with the West Bengal figures as estimated by the State Statistical Bureau (now the Bureau of Applied Economics and Statistics). In the first place, the Bureau's value-added figures are estimated net of depreciation whereas Bose's figures are gross of depreciation. Moreover, Bose's estimate of value added in manufacturing, based on the results of a 1962 CMPO census of manufacturing in the Calcutta Metropolitan District for which Bose was responsible, is considerably higher even net of depreciation than the estimate for manufacturing in the Bureau's value-added calculations[2], as is the estimate in Banerji's paper (see table 4). It is clear, nevertheless, that the bulk of value added from manufacturing, construction, transport and communications, and trade in West Bengal originates in the Calcutta Metropolitan District.

---

[1] At the time of completion of the present study, only the first set of preliminary figures from the 1971 Census had been published. See *Census of India, 1971*, Series 1: *India*, Paper 1 of 1971, Supplement: *Provisional population totals* (New Delhi, 1971), and Series 18: *West Bengal*, Paper 1 of 1971: *Provisional population totals* (Calcutta, 1971).

[2] A.N. Bose: *Implications of capacity utilisation*, op. cit., pp. 17-18.

Table 5.   Net value added by sector [1] in current prices in West Bengal, 1960/61, 1965/66, 1970/71

Sector	1960/61	1965/66	1970/71
A. *Rs crores*			
Agriculture and related activities	414	623	1 119
Mining	27	39	54
Manufacturing	234	394	416
Factory establishments	(175)	(325)	(337)
Small enterprises	(59)	(69)	(79)
Construction	15	16	18
Transport	63	82	98
Trade and services	338	453	599
Total net value added	1 091	1 607	2 304
B. *Percentages*			
Agriculture and related activities	38.0	38.8	48.6
Mining	2.5	2.4	2.4
Manufacturing	21.5	24.5	18.1
Factory establishments	(16.1)	(20.2)	(14.6)
Small enterprises	(5.4)	(4.3)	(3.5)
Construction	1.3	1.0	0.8
Transport	5.7	5.1	4.1
Trade and services	31.0	28.2	26.0
Total net value added	100.0	100.0	100.0

[1] Source does not indicate in which sector electric power is included.

Source: Derived from Government of West Bengal: *Economic review, year 1971-72*, op. cit., p. 68.

Some changes that have taken place in the structure of value added in West Bengal since 1960/61 are reflected in a new set of estimates by the Bureau of Applied Economics and Statistics published in 1972. [1] In 1960/61, 38 per cent of net value added in West Bengal originated in agriculture and related activities and 24 per cent in mining and manufacturing (see table 5). By 1965/66, the share of mining and manufacturing had risen to 26 per cent as a result of the expansion of the industrial economy during the first four years of the Third Five-Year Plan. In 1970/71, however, 49 per cent of West Bengal value added originated in agriculture and related activities and only 20 per cent in mining and manufacturing. In 1960/61, West Bengal accounted for 13 per cent of India's value added in manufacturing; in 1970/71, for only 9 per cent. [2] The economic crisis of metropolitan Calcutta in the latter part of the 1960s is summed up in these figures.

[1] Government of West Bengal: *Economic review, year 1971-72* (Calcutta, 1972), pp. 68-69.

[2] The percentage for 1970/71 is derived from preliminary figures of the Department of Statistics of the Government of India Central Statistical Office.

Table 6. Net value added, in selected sectors [1], at constant (1960/61) prices in West Bengal, 1960/61, 1965/66, 1970/71

Sector	1960/61	1965/66	1970/71
Rs crores			
Agriculture and related activities	414	395	474
Mining	27	32	30
Manufacturing	.	.	.
Factory establishments	(175)	(277)	(239)
Small enterprises	.	.	.
Index (1960/61 = 100)			
Agriculture and related activities	100.0	95.3	114.5
Mining	100.0	118.1	109.1
Manufacturing	.	.	.
Factory establishments	100.0	158.0	136.5
Small enterprises	.	.	.

[1] The only sectors for which the West Bengal Government Bureau of Applied Economics and Statistics prepares estimates of value added in constant prices are those shown in this table, and house property.

Source: Derived from Government of West Bengal: *Economic review, year 1971-72*, op. cit., p. 69.

The essential pattern appears more clearly in the annual constant price estimates prepared by the Bureau of Applied Economics and Statistics for income originating in selected sectors (table 6). The year 1965/66 saw the peak of the industrial boom in West Bengal and the immediate effect on agriculture of the first of the two drought years of the 1960s: that part of net value added in manufacturing which originated in factory establishments had risen by 58 per cent in real terms over the five-year period from 1960/61 to 1965/66 (i.e. at an average annual rate of growth of 9.6 per cent), while net value added in agriculture and related activities in 1965/66 was 5 per cent below its 1960/61 level. In 1970/71, net value added originating in factory establishments was down by 14 per cent from its 1965/66 peak (showing an average annual rate of decline of about 2.7 per cent over the second quinquennium of the decade). Agricultural value added in West Bengal recovered from the drought and in 1970/71 was 20 per cent above its 1965/66 trough in real terms (14 per cent above its 1960/61 level). The resulting 1.4 per cent average annual rate of increase in agricultural output over the decade was, however, much below the population growth rate.

Manufacturing

As the first centre of British capital in India, the Calcutta region had a head start on the rest of the country in the modern process of industrialisation. The first modern jute mills in India were set up in the 1870s in Baranagar, Budge Budge and Howrah, paper mills in the 1870s and 1880s, the first chemical and pharmaceutical works in the 1890s. The engineering industries of Howrah

Table 7. Employment, gross value of output, and net value added in manufacturing, all India, West Bengal and Bombay State or Maharashtra, 1948-68

Year	India			West Bengal			Bombay State or Maharashtra [1]			Source: Statistical Abstract of India	
	Employ-ment ('000)	Gross value of output (Rs crores)	Net value added (Rs crores)	Employ-ment ('000)	Gross value of output (Rs crores)	Net value added (Rs crores)	Employ-ment ('000)	Gross value of output (Rs crores)	Net value added (Rs crores)	Year	Pages
1948	1 704	953.6	317.3	535	272.6	75.2	574	340.7	142.0	1950	630-631
1949	1 685	976.1	272.7	515	268.8	66.6	565	333.5	113.6	1951-52	625-626
1950	1 632	1 028.0	283.9	.	.	.	.	.	.	1952-53	600-601
1951	1 633	1 306.9	347.2	475	355.8	90.7	538	456.1	137.2	1952-53	600-601
1952	1 648	1 184.0	315.0	473	309.8	85.0	544	410.8	113.7	1953-54	661-664
1953	1 628	1 122.8	334.2	452	257.0	80.8	541	400.0	126.0	1955-56	654-657
1954	1 715	1 287.5	372.9	465	291.0	93.3	538	418.2	131.6	1956-57	631-635
1955	1 786	1 409.2	442.1	488	338.3	102.1	551	440.4	148.6	1957-58	590-594
1956	1 886	1 614.3	468.7	495	374.2	112.2	627	536.3	171.3	1958-59	593-602
1957	1 813	1 640.2	444.6	456	368.7	104.4	564	523.2	150.4		
1958	1 709	1 611.8	463.5	463	386.7	122.7	494	486.7	149.3	1961	105-109
1959	2 870	2 691.4	813.4	662	598.0	187.6	607	668.6	214.6	1962	121-123
1960	2 904	3 150.4	864.4	665	720.4	193.1	626	777.3	238.3	1963 & 1964	123-125
1961	3 050	3 693.4	977.6	679	814.2	204.3	650	903.1	266.4		
1962	3 268	4 176.3	1 115.4	729	944.3	252.0	674	1 019.7	309.6	1965	122-124
1963	3 448	4 798.8	1 295.0	794	1 094.6	296.4	690	1 178.8	341.6	1966	106-108
1964	3 804	5 626.3	1 501.1	825	1 207.3	330.4	755	1 367.5	384.3	1967	105-107
1965	3 986	6 501.7	1 707.0	880	1 378.0	355.9	767	1 540.5	424.7	1968	125-127
1966	3 934	7 212.7	1 810.0	863	1 433.8	352.3	746	1 756.3	470.2		
1967	.	.	.	822	1 429.2	353.7	.	.	.	.	.
1968	.	.	.	746	1 299.9	335.9	.	.	.	.	.

[1] 1948-1958: Bombay State; 1959-1966: Maharashtra (about 300,000 sq. km of the former Bombay State, the remaining 200,000 or so in the north-west forming the new state of Gujarat).

Sources: 1948-1965: Government of India, Central Statistical Organisation: Statistical abstract of India (New Delhi, annual), as indicated in the last two columns of the table. 1966: Government of India, Department of Statistics, Central Statistical Organisation (Industrial Statistics Wing): Annual survey of industries 1966, census sector (provisional results), general review (Calcutta, 1969), pp. 13, 59, 89. 1967: (West Bengal): Ibid.: Annual survey of industries 1967, census sector (provisional results), general review (Calcutta, 1970), p. 123. 1968 (West BengaD): Government of West Bengal, State Planning Board.

Table 8.   Employment, gross value of output, and net value added in manufacturing: West Bengal and Bombay State or Maharashtra as share of all India, 1948-66 (Percentages)

Year	Employment		Gross value of output		Net value added by manufacture	
	West Bengal	Bombay State or Maharashtra [1]	West Bengal	Bombay State or Maharashtra [1]	West Bengal	Bombay State or Maharashtra [1]
1948	31.4	33.7	28.6	35.7	23.7	44.8
1949	30.6	33.5	27.5	34.2	24.4	41.7
1950	.	.	.		.	
1951	29.1	32.9	27.2	34.9	26.1	39.5
1952	28.7	33.0	26.2	34.7	27.0	36.1
1953	27.8	33.2	22.9	35.6	24.2	37.7
1954	27.1	31.4	22.6	32.5	25.0	35.3
1955	27.3	30.9	24.0	31.3	23.1	33.6
1956	26.2	33.2	23.2	33.2	23.9	36.5
1957	25.2	31.1	22.5	31.9	23.5	33.8
1958	27.1	28.9	24.0	32.0	26.5	32.2
1959	23.1	21.1	22.2	24.8	23.1	26.4
1960	22.9	21.6	22.9	24.7	22.3	27.6
1961	22.3	21.3	22.0	24.5	20.9	27.3
1962	22.3	20.6	22.6	24.4	22.6	27.6
1963	23.0	20.0	22.8	24.6	22.9	26.4
1964	21.7	19.8	21.5	24.3	22.0	25.6
1965	22.1	19.2	21.2	23.7	20.8	24.9
1966	21.9	19.0	19.9	24.4	19.5	26.0

[1] 1948-1958: Bombay State; 1959-1966: Maharashtra.

Source: Derived from table 7.

had their beginnings in the 1870s. Coal and iron mines were developed on a large scale in Calcutta's hinterland in the 1860s and 1870s.[1]

In 1921, over one-third of India's industrial workers were in Bengal Province[2], while Bombay Province contained one-fourth. In 1939, the shares of the two Provinces stood at 29 per cent for Bengal Province and 23 per cent for Bombay Province.[3] In 1948, after Partition and Independence, West Bengal accounted for 31 per cent and Bombay State for 34 per cent of employment in large-scale manufacturing in India, i.e. factories covered by the "census sector"

[1] Bengal Chamber of Commerce and Industry: *West Bengal*, An analytical study (New Delhi, Bombay and Calcutta, Oxford and IBH Publishing Co., 1971), pp. 9-10.

[2] With the partition of India in 1947, the western part of Bengal Province became the Indian Union's State of West Bengal, while the eastern part went to the newly constituted State of Pakistan (as East Pakistan).

[3] Bengal Chamber of Commerce and Industry: *West Bengal*, op. cit., p. 90, quoting Government of India: *Location of industry in India* (New Delhi, 1945).

of the Central Statistical Office's Annual Survey of Industries. According to that source, employment in manufacturing in Bombay State continued to exceed that of West Bengal until 1958 (see table 7). In 1959, with the reorganisation of the state boundaries and the creation of Maharashtra, West Bengal regained first place in terms of manufacturing employment. Total gross value of output of manufacturing and net value added by manufacture in Bombay State or Maharashtra, on the other hand, have exceeded West Bengal's throughout the post-Independence period. Although the percentage shares both of West Bengal on the one hand and of Bombay State or Maharashtra on the other have fallen with the development of newer centres of industrialisation in other states (see table 8), West Bengal still accounted in 1966 for 22 per cent of India's total employment in the census sector of manufacturing and for 20 per cent of both gross value of manufacturing output and net value added by manufacture.

The two leading industries in West Bengal, both of which are concentrated in metropolitan Calcutta, are jute manufactures and engineering. Within India, jute manufacturing is almost entirely located in West Bengal. The engineering industry is much more widely dispersed, but 30 per cent of it in terms of employment, 28 per cent in terms of gross value of output and 28 per cent in terms of value added by manufacture were located in West Bengal in 1965, the peak year for industrial employment in that state.

Until the late 1950s, jute manufacturing was the predominant industry in West Bengal. The number of its employed workers reached a peak of 347,000 in 1930/31, and still stood at as many as 315,000 in 1948/49.[1] With the increasing post-Partition difficulties in obtaining raw jute supplies from East Pakistan and with increasing competition from new jute mills there, the number of workers employed in the West Bengal jute mills fell steadily to a low point of 202,000 in 1961 (see table 9). There was a sharp recovery to 259,000 in 1965 and again a steady decline which started with a sharp fall in raw jute production in 1965/66 because of the drought. By 1969, the number of workers in jute manufacturing had fallen back to 204,000. The difficulties of the jute industry have been cumulative: with each poor crop that has reduced the supply of raw jute and with each industrial dispute that has interrupted the flow of jute manufactures, a piece of the world market for jute products has been lost to synthetic substitutes.

Jute manufacturing lost its position as West Bengal's leading industrial employer in 1959, when employment fell to 210,000 in registered factories in jute manufacturing and rose to 221,000 in the engineering industries (table 9).

---

[1] S. N. Sen and Tapan Piplai: *Industrial relations in the jute industry in West Bengal*, A case study (Calcutta, Bookland, 1968), pp. 11-14.

Table 9.   Workers employed in registered factories in West Bengal, 1951-70

Year	Number ('000)				As percentages of number in all industries	
	All industries	Jute textiles	Engin-eering	Others	Jute textiles	Engin-eering
1951	652	278	158	216	42.6	24.2
1952	622	268	157	197	43.1	25.2
1953	608	252	153	203	41.4	25.2
1954	611	252	157	202	41.2	25.7
1955	647	252	181	214	38.9	28.0
1956	659	254	182	223	38.5	27.6
1957	668	236	198	234	35.3	29.6
1958	668	221	210	237	33.1	31.4
1959	675	210	221	244	31.1	32.7
1960	704	213	236	255	30.2	33.5
1961	718	202	250	266	28.1	34.8
1962	771	229	271	271	29.7	35.1
1963	817	240	204	373	29.4	25.0
1964	854	251	303	300	29.4	35.5
1965	880	259	324	297	29.4	36.8
1966	840	230	319	291	27.4	38.0
1967	832	232	310	290	27.9	37.3
1968	817	222	301	294	27.2	36.8
1969	791	204	295	292	25.8	37.3
1970	809	.	.	.	.	.

Sources: 1951-1969: Calcutta Metropolitan Planning Organisation: *A note on the economic development programme for the Calcutta Metropolitan District*, op. cit., 1970 (all industries). Government of West Bengal: *Economic review, year 1971-72*, op. cit., p. 98.

Thereafter, jute regained its leading position only once, in 1963, when jute was midway through a brief period of rapid recovery between 1961 and 1965 whereas engineering experienced a sharp one-year drop. At the 1965 peak of industrial activity in West Bengal, the number of workers reached 259,000 in jute manufacturing and 324,000 in the engineering industries. These two major sectors together accounted for 66 per cent of workers in all registered factories in West Bengal.

During the decade and a half of industrial expansion under the first three Five-Year Plans, the engineering industry markedly increased its share of workers in all registered factories in West Bengal—from 24 per cent in 1951 to 37 per cent in 1965. During the downturn in activity in the second half of the 1960s, engineering more or less maintained its share of the declining total of factory workers since jute was affected even more severely.

Small enterprises in engineering are usually subcontractors for larger enterprises (e.g. in the case of radio components). There are, however, direct government purchases from small-scale industry (e.g. locks).

Table 10. Engineering industry (census sector) by branch, India and West Bengal, 1965: productive capital, employment, gross value of output and net value added

Branch	A. Productive capital [1]			B. Employment		
	Rs crores		W. Bengal as % of India (2)÷(1)	'000		W. Bengal as % of India (5)÷(4)
	India (1)	West Bengal (2)	(3)	India (4)	West Bengal (5)	(6)
Basic metals	1 252.4	408.4	32.6	329	118	35.9
Metal products	96.3	33.0	34.3	91	31	34.1
General machinery	264.4	62.4	23.6	196	48	24.5
Electrical machinery	234.3	37.9	16.2	142	37	26.1
Transport equipment	356.5	89.8	25.2	415	115	27.7
Scientific instruments	15.2	3.1	20.4	14	3	21.4
Total	2 219.1	634.6	28.6	1 187	352	29.6

Branch	C. Gross value of output			D. Net value added by manufacture		
	Rs crores		W. Bengal as % of India (8)÷(7)	Rs crores		W. Bengal as % of India (11)÷(10)
	India (7)	West Bengal (8)	(9)	India (10)	West Bengal (11)	(12)
Basic metals	833.8	242.5	29.1	198.0	60.9	30.8
Metal products	169.3	60.8	35.9	47.8	18.0	37.7
General machinery	279.0	63.9	22.9	92.3	21.9	23.7
Electrical machinery	278.6	79.8	28.6	80.5	22.3	27.7
Transport equipment	545.6	134.6	24.7	168.0	40.9	24.3
Scientific instruments	14.0	3.1	22.1	5.5	1.5	27.3
Total	2 120.3	584.7	27.6	592.1	165.5	28.0

[1] Productive capital = fixed capital *plus* working capital.

Source: Government of India, Central Statistical Organisation (Industrial Statistics Wing): *Annual survey of industries 1966, census sector (provisional results), general review*, op. cit., pp. 9, 11, 87, 89.

According to the annual survey of industries in the census sector that is carried out by the Central Statistical Organisation, total employment (factory workers plus supervisory and managerial personnel) in West Bengal's engineering industry reached a peak of 352,000, or 40 per cent of employment in all manufacturing industry, in 1965. Value added per person employed in engineering being high, in that year it accounted for 47 per cent of value added in all manufacturing. In the same year, engineering accounted for 51 per cent of productive capital (fixed plus working capital) invested in all manufacturing.

West Bengal accounted in 1965 for around one-third of India's productive capital in the basic metals and metal products branches of engineering and for over a third of India's employment in these branches (see table 10). In the

Table 11. Capital, output, and value added per person employed in manufacturing (all industries, engineering, and other), West Bengal, 1959, 1965, 1967

A. Absolute amounts

Item	All industries			Engineering			Other		
	1959	1965	1967	1959	1965	1967	1959	1965	1967
Rs crores (= Rs 10 m.)									
1. Productive capital	377.1	1 247.9	1 453.7	160.1	634.6	793.8	217.0	613.3	659.9
2. Gross value of output	598.0	1 278.0	1 429.2	•	584.7	534.7	•	693.3	894.5
3. Net value added	187.6	355.9	353.7	70.3	165.5	142.5	117.3	190.4	211.2
Number ('000)									
4. Employment	662	880	822	215	352	326	•	528	496
Rupees									
5. Productive capital per employee (1) ÷ (4)	5 696.4	14 180.7	17 684.9	7 446.5	18 028.4	24 349.7	4 854.6	11 615.5	13 304.4
6. Gross value of output per employee (2) ÷ (4)	9 033.2	14 522.7	17 386.9	9 744.2	16 610.8	16 401.8	8 691.3	13 130.7	18 034.3
7. Net value added per employee (3) ÷ (4)	2 833.8	4 044.3	4 302.9	3 269.8	4 701.7	4 371.2	2 624.2	3 606.1	4 258.1
8. Gross value of output per unit of productive capital (2) ÷ (1)	1.586	1.024	0.983	5.308	0.921	0.674	1.790	1.130	1.356
9. Net value added per unit of productive capital (3) ÷ (1)	0.497	0.285	0.243	0.439	0.261	0.180	0.541	0.310	0.320

B. Average annual growth rates
(percentages)

Item	All industries		Engineering		Other	
	1959 to 1965	1965 to 1967	1959 to 1965	1965 to 1967	1959 to 1965	1965 to 1967
1. Productive capital	22.6	7.9	25.8	11.8	19.0	3.7
2. Gross value of output	12.7	5.7	18.7	4.4	10.1	13.5
3. Net value added	10.7	–0.3	15.3	7.2	8.2	5.3
4. Employment	4.9	3.4	8.6	3.8	2.8	3.1
5. Productive capital per employee	16.4	11.7	15.9	16.0	15.2	7.2
6. Gross value of output per employee	8.3	9.4	9.3	0.6	7.1	17.0
7. Net value added per employee	6.2	3.6	6.2	3.6	5.4	8.7
8. Gross value of output per unit of productive capital	–7.0	–2.0	–2.7	–14.5	8.8	3.5
9. Net value added per unit of productive capital	–8.9	–7.7	–8.5	–17.0	9.1	1.5

Sources: 1959: All industries: Government of India, Central Statistical Organisation: *Statistical abstract of the Indian Union, 1962* (New Delhi, 1962), pp. 120-123. Engineering: Data supplied by Dr. D. Biswas of CMPO, on the basis of Central Statistical Organisation (Industrial Statistics Wing): *Annual survey of industries, 1959.* 1965: Government of India, Central Statistical Organisation (Industrial Statistics Wing): *Annual survey of industries 1966, census sector* (provisional results), general review, op. cit., pp. 86-89. 1967: Idem: *Annual survey of industries 1967, census sector* (provisional results) general review (Calcutta, 1972, mimeographed), pp. 120-123.

case of the electrical machinery branch, West Bengal accounted for only 16 per cent of India's productive capital but for 26 per cent of employment.

During the period of rapid industrial expansion from 1959 to 1965, value added at current prices in all manufacturing (census sector) in West Bengal increased much faster than employment. This was due partly to intervening price rises and partly to increases in real productivity per person employed such as might be expected in view of the even faster increase in capital stock (also valued at current prices).[1] Employment in all of manufacturing rose from 1959 to 1965 by 5 per cent per year, net value added (at current prices) by 11 per cent per year and the capital stock by 23 per cent per year; in the engineering industry, the average annual growth rates were 9 per cent for employment, 15 per cent for net value added (at current prices) and 26 per cent for productive capital (see table 11). Net value added per unit of productive capital correspondingly declined by 8.9 per cent per year in all manufacturing and by 8.5 per cent per year in the engineering industry.

During the first two years of the post-1965 recession, as registered by the annual survey of industries in the census sector for 1967, value added in all manufacturing in West Bengal declined a little despite the intervening rise in prices, while employment fell by 3.4 per cent per year. In the engineering industry the decline in value added (7.2 per cent per year) was much more marked than in manufacturing as a whole, whereas the decline in employment was only a little faster (3.8 per cent per year). The rate of growth in the capital stock continued to be considerably faster in engineering than in all of manufacturing, so that the decline in value added per unit of capital was much sharper in engineering (17 per cent per year) than in all of manufacturing, reflecting a sharp increase in the rate of under-utilisation of capacity.

The two smallest branches of West Bengal's engineering industry—metal products and scientific instruments—showed the highest rates of growth in net value added (at current prices) during the 1959-1965 period of industrial expansion: 29 per cent per year for metal products and 22 per cent for scientific instruments (see table 12). In the three other main branches, the growth rates were lower than in the engineering industry in India as a whole. The employment increase was highest in the metal products branch. Over the first two years of the downturn (from 1965 to 1967), the decline in value added was sharpest in general machinery (26 per cent per year), followed by basic metals (15 per cent per year). There was no decline in employment in the general machinery branch, although basic metals and metal products showed declines of, respectively, 9.3 per cent and 6.7 per cent per year.

---

[1] CMPO, Industrial Planning Team: *Report on the engineering industry*, op. cit., p. 10. The report used preliminary figures for 1965. The revised Annual Survey of Industries figures for 1965 have been used in table 11.

Table 12. Engineering industry (census sector) by branch, India and West Bengal, employment and net value added, 1959, 1965, 1967

A. Employment

Branch	Absolute numbers (thousands)			Average annual rate of increase (per cent)	
	1959	1965	1967	1959 to 1965	1965 to 1967
India					
Basic materials	171	329	.	10.9	.
Metal products	43	91	.	12.6	.
General machinery	80	196	.	15.1	.
Electrical machinery	65	142	.	13.1	.
Transport equipment	263	415	.	7.9	.
Scientific instruments	5	14	.	17.3	.
Total	627	1 187	.	10.7	.
West Bengal					
Basic metals	.	118	97	7.0	—9.3
Metal products	.	31	27	15.9	—6.7
General machinery	.	48	48	11.0	—
Electrical machinery	.	37	35	7.0	—2.7
Transport equipment	.	115	116 }	5.5	{ 0.4
Scientific instruments	.	3	3 }		{ —
Total	.	352	326	7.5	—3.8

B. Net value added at current prices

Branch	Absolute figures (Rs crores)			Average annual rate of increase (per cent)	
	1959	1965	1967	1959 to 1965	1965 to 1967
India					
Basic metals	64.9	198.0	.	20.2	.
Metal products	13.6	47.8	.	23.4	.
General machinery	22.0	92.3	.	27.0	.
Electrical machinery	25.9	80.5	.	20.8	.
Transport equipment	68.9	168.0	.	14.9	.
Scientific instruments	1.6	5.5	.	20.4	.
Total	196.9	592.1	.	18.5	.
West Bengal					
Basic metals	26.3	60.9	43.4	14.1	—15.6
Metal products	3.3	18.0	13.2	28.6	—14.4
General machinery	7.3	21.9	12.2	18.5	—25.8
Electrical machinery	10.7	22.3	26.9	12.4	9.8
Transport equipment	22.3	40.9	45.2	10.6	5.1
Scientific instruments	0.4	1.5	1.6	22.2	3.3
Total	70.3	165.5	142.5	14.3	—7.2

Sources: 1959: India: Government of India, Central Statistical Organisation: *Statistical abstract of the Indian Union 1962*, op. cit., p. 125. West Bengal: employment: West Bengal State Planning Board; net value added: CMPO, Industrial Planning Team: *Report on the engineering industry, West Bengal, 1951-1968* Calcutta, 1968), p. 5, derived from Central Statistical Organisation (Industrial Statistics Wing): *Annual survey of industries 1959*. 1965: Government of India, Central Statistical Organisation (Industrial Statistics Wing): *Annual survey of industries 1966, census sector (provisional results), general review*, op. cit., pp. 87, 89. 1967: West Bengal: Idem: *Annual survey of industries 1967, census sector (provisional results), general review*, op. cit., pp. 120-122.

Trade, services and the informal sector

As noted above (in table 3), transport, construction, trade and services occupied in 1961 over one-half of the working population of the Calcutta Metropolitan District but only about 16 per cent of the rest of West Bengal's. Transport, trade, and services were the sectors of origin of some 42 per cent of the net value added estimated for metropolitan Calcutta in 1961 and of some 37 per cent for all of West Bengal in 1960/61 (table 4). With the growth in total net value added over the decade, the share of total estimated net value added of West Bengal originating in transport, trades and services fell to 33 per cent by 1965/66 and to 31 per cent in 1970/71 (table 5). However, without access to the underlying assumptions concerning employment and unit output used by the Bureau of Applied Economics and Statistics it is difficult to judge how much of this shift is real and how much of it might be an estimating illusion.

Current statistics on employment in the organised sector of the transport and trade-and-services groups are sparse and their coverage is limited (see chapter 3 below). The general impression they give is of a gradual expansion of activity in trade, in transport and in government services over the decade of the 1960s but at too slow a rate to absorb much of the expanding labour force. Within metropolitan Calcutta, the growth of public transport activity was limited by the saturation of the capacity of existing inner city mass transit facilities, the shortage of foreign exchange for the purchase of buses and the poor state of repair of, and lack of improvement in, the street and highway system. Suburban rail activity, on the other hand, expanded with increased commuting from areas as far away from Calcutta as Burdwan. Goods traffic into, out of and within the industrial areas of metropolitan Calcutta continued to expand at least throughout the period of industrial development that ended in 1965.

Owing to the financial difficulties of the Calcutta Corporation and the other local authorities of the Calcutta Metropolitan District, there was little expansion of municipal government services. On the other hand, state and central government services expanded steadily throughout the decade.[1]

Banking and financial services also expanded but were adversely affected in the late 1960s by a tendency on the part of a number of business firms to leave Calcutta for less troubled centres elsewhere in India. A temporary but severe setback to Calcutta's role as a centre of financial and business

---

[1] See Chapter 3 below; and *Employment trends in West Bengal*, Background Paper II, Seminar on growth of employment opportunities, Indian Chamber of Commerce, Calcutta, 5 May 1972.

services occurred in 1969 with the abolition of the managing agencies[1], which is said to have resulted in the disappearance of 50,000 jobs from Calcutta although many of these must have been replaced by openings in the successor firms.

Information on the unorganised or informal sector of metropolitan Calcutta's urban economy is at best obtainable only indirectly. It is, for example, possible to estimate employment in the informal sector from census data or from household survey data, but only as a residual between the census or survey aggregates and administrative data obtained on a regular basis directly from enterprises and government entities. By their very nature, the constituents of the informal sector do not lend themselves to direct quantification because of smallness of scale, lack of formal registration or licensing and often the lack of a fixed place of activity. There is some coverage of small-scale industry in the sample sector of the Central Statistical Organisation's annual survey of industries and in the administrative records of the Directorate of Cottage and Small-Scale Industries. There are also some hints in the labour force surveys cited in chapter 3 below on the extent of occupations in what might be called the urban subsistence economy. Essentially, however, the informal sector is characterised by an absence of statistics. Especially the minor services—casual labour, porterage, rickshaw pulling, domestic services, petty trade and street hawking—which absorb perhaps 40 per cent of the urban working population, are essentially uncounted and their output is extremely difficult, if not impossible, to measure. For that matter, a question of national accounting theory that arises is whether the incomes earned from some of the more dubious activities in the informal sector—such as begging, prostitution and theft—represent "productive" income or merely income transfers.

One of the more paradoxical aspects of the activities carried out in the informal sector is that their growth may represent a reaction either to a general economic expansion or to a general economic contraction. An expansion of the organised sectors of the urban economy generates additional incomes which attract suppliers of the minor services. On the other hand, by throwing people out of employment in the organised sectors or blocking their absorption if they are new arrivals on the urban labour market, a contraction forces addi-

---

[1] The abolition came into effect on 3 April 1970 (see the Companies (Amendment) Act, section 4, in *Gazette of India, Extraordinary*, 29 May 1969). Previously any Indian limited company operating in the private sector of industry or commerce might vest powers of management of its business in a "managing agent"—that is, in an individual or a firm or a body corporate who or which, by virtue of a contract with the company, undertook in consideration of remuneration the management of the company's affairs subject to the control of the company's board of directors. See F. Chalmers Wright: *Licensed delegation of company management in India, with special reference to the "managing agency" system* (Calcutta, Bengal Chamber of Commerce and Industry, 1959).

tional members of the labour force into the subsistence service activities mentioned above. As suggested by A. Ghosh, the statistical factor that most directly explains growth of the tertiary sector in Calcutta is growth of the population itself.[1] The obvious reason is that it is in the unorganised tertiary sector that the residual members of the urban labour force find their livelihood. At the same time, the over-all concentration of population in any metropolis represents a greater concentration of demand for casual labour of all sorts and a larger market for petty trade and services than are to be found anywhere else.

PROSPECTS FOR THE 1970s

Calcutta's development possibilities in 1972 were better than they had been for a decade as the result of a combination of events which improved morale and gave an optimistic tone to the city's future prospects: the creation of Bangladesh at Calcutta's doorstep; political stability due to President's rule[2], which was imposed in West Bengal in 1970; the overwhelming victory of the Congress Party in the state elections held in West Bengal on 11 March 1972; and a flurry of activity by the Calcutta Metropolitan Development Authority (CMDA) since its establishment under President's rule in 1970. On the one hand, improved morale and political stability are essential in a social situation that was marked for several years by growing unemployment, political violence and a rash of disruptive labour-management disputes in Calcutta's industrial belt. On the other hand, the establishment of Bangladesh at least temporarily creates increased demands on Calcutta's industrial output to meet that country's need both for a variety of consumer goods previously imported from West Pakistan and for the physical reconstruction of its transport network (most of it financed by the Government of India).

Political stability and economic growth

Two positive effects of political stability have already occurred. One of them, which was reinforced by an industrial truce agreed to by the trade unions and employers during the Indo-Pakistan war in December 1971, has been a sharp reduction in industrial unrest in West Bengal. The other has been a reduction of the physical violence which, by scaring away entre-

---

[1] *Census of India, 1961*, Monograph Series, Monograph No. 2: *Calcutta—the primate city*, by A. Ghosh (New Delhi, 1966), p. 51.

[2] Direct government by the Government of India in an Indian state.

preneurs and managers reluctant to live under a daily threat of physical intimidation, served to accelerate capital flight from West Bengal and Calcutta during the late 1960s.

The main positive effect of political stability both in West Bengal and in the government of the Indian Union has been, however, that there is now a prospect that government and private investment activity will be stepped up. A major revival of investment activity by the Government of India and by the public sector enterprises, particularly the railways, would result in a marked increase in the level of demand for the products of metropolitan Calcutta's engineering industries. The recent establishment of a State Planning Board for West Bengal should lead to increased investment activity in the state, if only because a coherent state plan will strengthen West Bengal's position in lobbying for investment funds from the Government of India.

A sustained period of political stability will also tend to encourage a general expansion of Calcutta's economy, particularly if accompanied by a high level of government development expenditures on urban infrastructure. Increased activity in manufacturing will automatically create new jobs both directly in industry and indirectly in the services that grow up around industrial activity. Any easing of the over-all problem of employment creation will permit a concentration of employment policy on the specific problems that lead to political instability.

Bangladesh

The opening of the border between Bangladesh and West Bengal in December 1971 reopened a brisk border trade in consumer goods, with fish being imported into West Bengal and cigarettes, matches and cooking oil being exported to Bangladesh. Although there were some immediate price rises in West Bengal as manufactured goods were syphoned off into Bangladesh, the price of fish, one of the staples of Calcutta's diet, which had been in short supply since Partition, tumbled down.

Reconstruction of the war-damaged railway systems of Bangladesh was expected to create an immediate market for Indian railway wagons, locomotives and other railway material. By the spring of 1972 Calcutta's engineering firms had received enquiries (but no firm orders) for bridge structurals, railway wagons, jute machinery and tea estate machinery for Bangladesh. It was expected that Bangladesh would import from India other engineering items required for physical reconstruction, as well as cement, coal, fertilisers and other textiles. An effort is being made by the Governments of India and Bangladesh to channel as much of the trade as possible through their respective state trading corporations.

In the medium term, Bangladesh will continue to require industrial goods produced by metropolitan Calcutta but will be faced with the problem of finding the resources to pay for them. In the longer term, Bangladesh will have to step up its own industrialisation and it is not certain whether the resulting production pattern will be complementary to or competitive with West Bengal's. Textiles will eventually be produced in Bangladesh, while India is encouraging development of the Chittagong steel rolling mill.

In the very short run, West Bengal's jute manufactures and exports benefited from the chaotic events in East Pakistan. During the 1971 civil war in East Pakistan which led up to the independence of Bangladesh, East Pakistan's production of raw jute and exports of jute manufactures suffered severe setbacks, while West Bengal's production and exports of jute manufactures rose in partial compensation.

This situation may continue for a while. The Bangladesh jute industry's troubles are likely to continue for some time because of the ownership and management pattern of the industry, on the one hand, and the composition of the industrial labour force, on the other. As in West Bengal, ownership and management of the jute mills were to a considerable extent non-Bengali; and, again as in West Bengal, the labour force was to a considerable extent composed of Bihari Muslims. Expulsion of the West Pakistan management from Bangladesh and ill treatment of the Biharis in the wake of the East Pakistan civil war will delay recovery of the jute industry in Bangladesh.

In the medium term, the creation of Bangladesh is likely to improve somewhat the supply position of West Bengal's jute manufacturing industry. One effect of the newly re-established closer economic relations between the two Bengals should be to facilitate the supply of Bangladesh raw jute to the West Bengal mills. To the extent, however, that all of Bengal is subject to the same climatic conditions, raw jute production in Bangladesh and production in West Bengal fluctuate together; raw jute shortages will appear at the same time in both areas.

In the longer term, the predominance of the two Bengals in total world production of jute could enable them, through joint marketing and avoidance of competitive price cutting, to maximise their total receipts. Maintainance of that predominance in the world market, however, will require substantial expansion of raw jute production in the two Bengals at prices competitive with synthetic substitutes.

Agricultural growth and the expansion of manufacturing

One of the key factors in the future expansion of the economy of metropolitan Calcutta will be the rate of growth of agriculture in West Bengal.

West Bengal's agriculture traditionally supplies metropolitan Calcutta with both wage goods (particularly food grains) and raw materials (mainly jute). Expansion of West Bengal's agricultural production in the 1970s will ease the supply position for metropolitan Calcutta. Substantial increases in food grains production, by holding down the price of the major component of low-income budgets, can be a significant factor in restraining demands for wage increases and in thereby holding down industrial production costs.

At the same time, the development of rural West Bengal should play an important role in providing a market for the industrial goods produced by metropolitan Calcutta. Any strategy for the regeneration of Calcutta will be closely linked to the agricultural development of West Bengal.[1] Whereas rural West Bengal's backward agriculture now slows down the growth of Calcutta's economy, its accelerated development, which can result only from the rapid spread of tube wells, pumps and agricultural equipment, will create increasing demands for the products of metropolitan Calcutta, and particularly of its engineering industries.

An encouraging aspect of the situation lies in the fact that the technological advances which have brought the Green Revolution to other parts of India have begun to take hold in West Bengal as well. Wheat plantings in West Bengal expanded rapidly during the three most recent years of good monsoons, rising from 240,000 hectares in 1969/70 to 320,000 hectares in 1970/71 and to 470,000 hectares in 1971/72; and it was expected that 1 million hectares would soon be under wheat. In 1971, average wheat yields in West Bengal reached 2,441 kg per hectare, which in India is an amount second only to that reached in Punjab State. Although rice production has made no striking advances, registering only small increases in average yields since 1964/65, yields of dry-season rice (*boro* rice, which is planted between November and February and harvested in May and June before the monsoon) rose rapidly in 1971, the degree of water control permitted by irrigation making it possible to use the new rice strains. The spread of dry-season irrigation through the use of tube wells has also brought with it some experimental plantings of short-staple cotton as an off-season crop in the 24-Parganas District.

The degree of success of multiple cropping in West Bengal based on dry-season irrigation will depend on the rate at which the use of tube wells spreads. Increasing the number of tube wells will not only increase agricultural production; it will also improve drainage and reduce waterlogging. Tube wells are therefore one of rural West Bengal's most urgent needs, and the West

---

[1] See Government of West Bengal, Calcutta Metropolitan Planning Organisation: *A memorandum on a perspective plan for Calcutta Metropolitan District and West Bengal, 1971-1989* (Calcutta, 1971).

Bengal State Planning Board has recently proposed a comprehensive area development programme[1] designed to introduce tube wells into rural West Bengal on a large scale.

The spread of tube well use in West Bengal is bound to lead to increased demands on the under-utilised capacity of the Calcutta-Howrah engineering industries. According to R. D. Vidyarthi, Secretary of the Engineering Association of India, some pumps are at present produced in metropolitan Calcutta but tube well equipment comes in from other industrial areas of India; there is no diesel engine factory in Calcutta. Part of the explanation for the lack of production of motor-driven water-lift equipment is that the water table in most of West Bengal is high. Furthermore, West Bengal has generally been content with the traditional practice of single-crop agriculture using lift irrigation from the rivers, so that the demand for underground water has been limited. Any substantial increase in local demand for tube well equipment and diesel pump sets will induce the versatile metal-working factories and workshops of Calcutta and Howrah to produce them.

Demand and supply constraints

The expansion of manufacturing in metropolitan Calcutta is hampered by insufficiency of demand for the products of some traditional industries, by shortages of raw materials for some others and by difficulties in securing the capital required for establishing newer and more dynamic industries.

The most severe fall in demand during the post-1965 recession concerned two of Calcutta's major engineering specialties, namely heavy castings and structurals. In early 1972 these sectors were still faced with lack of demand; but once demand increases become effective, expansion of production will be hampered by India's persistent steel shortage. Overcoming that shortage will involve either solving a longer-run problem of increasing the efficiency of management and improving labour-management relations in the steel industry so that the existing steel plants can operate closer to capacity, or finding additional sources of foreign exchange for larger imports of steel. India's steel shortage is likely to continue for several years at least.

It should be noted in passing that the engineering industry was one sector whose output recovered significantly in 1971 despite sluggishness of demand for heavy castings and structurals. The rise in output had little immediate effect on employment in engineering, however, because most of the enterprises in West Bengal which remained in operation throughout the recession

---

[1] Government of West Bengal, State Planning Board: *Comprehensive Area Development Programme (CADP): A new strategy for development* (Calcutta, 1973).

had been under pressure not to retrench, and remained overstaffed. With surplus manpower carried by many firms since 1966, the initial recovery in activity in 1971 resulted in fuller utilisation of the existing work force and little fresh recruitment.

Shortage of raw jute have been a persistent cause of falling production of jute manufactures in metropolitan Calcutta. A joint production programme with Bangladesh will alleviate this particular shortage to some extent, as will increasing jute yields resulting from modernisation of agriculture.

Demand for electronic products, one of the newer branches within the engineering industry, is expanding, but the sector is a novel one for Calcutta and has to be built up from scratch.

Calcutta's chemical and pharmaceutical industries, which were pioneers in India, are based on traditional raw materials, alcohol and coke. The currently expanding chemical industries in India are those based on petrochemicals and are concentrated in Bombay, which has had access to a local supply of petrochemical raw materials for a decade and a half. The Calcutta area's first petrochemical complex is yet to be created at Haldia, where a petroleum refinery is under construction close to the new port[1] and a fertiliser plant is planned. The Haldia refinery will send naphtha to the fertiliser plant in Durgapur while the Haldia fertiliser plant will import its raw materials. A local supply of petrochemicals for the manufacture of plastics and for other uses in metropolitan Calcutta is therefore still some years off.

---

[1] See below, Annex B, p. 116.

MIGRATION, EMPLOYMENT AND UNEMPLOYMENT

3

The view has been expressed that the magnitude of the urban employment problem in the developing countries stems from a rate of rural-urban migration that far exceeds the capacity of the urban economy to absorb the resulting increases in the urban labour force.[1] In a first part of the present chapter, the relevance of this explanation to Calcutta's situation is examined and the effect of migration to Calcutta on the local labour force and employment patterns is assessed. The other parts of the chapter are devoted to an examination in some detail of the structure of employment and of the nature and extent of unemployment in metropolitan Calcutta.

MIGRATION

The size of the working population in metropolitan Calcutta is affected by two kinds of migration flows—on the one hand seasonal immigration and emigration, and on the other inflows of persons seeking to settle for longer periods. To the extent, however, that workers who reside in metropolitan Calcutta without their families may return to their places of origin for considerable stretches of time in the course of the year, these two categories of migratory movement may overlap.

So far as seasonal movements are concerned, appreciable numbers of Calcutta's pavement-dwelling unskilled labourers[2] are known to return to their villages early in December in time for the harvest and to start coming back

---

[1] Bairoch: *Urban unemployment in developing countries*, op. cit. Although (as will be shown) the influx of migrants is a primary cause of the rapid growth of Calcutta's population, it should not be overlooked that the rate of natural population growth is high enough to exercise by itself a considerable influence on the problems that Calcutta will have to face between now and the end of the century.

[2] Estimates of the number of persons sleeping on the streets of Calcutta—either because they have no shelter or because it is cooler than indoors—vary from 40,000 to 200,000 depending on the season.

to the city after mid-January. This seasonal outflow, coupled with visits to families in the rural areas, seems likely to provide the rural sources of labour supply with a rather effective network of information on the Calcutta labour market.[1]

One of the main characteristics of the Calcutta working force noted in all the population and labour force surveys of the city is its complex geographical origin. For that matter, Calcutta has been a city of immigrants ever since its foundation. Nevertheless, the rate of immigration has been falling. In India as a whole, there was a marked slowing down of the rate of rural-urban migration from 1951 to 1961, partly as a result of saturation of at least the central portions of several large Indian cities[2], while in the case of Calcutta there has apparently been a considerable further slowing down in the rate of immigration since 1961. The small increase between 1961 and 1971 in the ratio of urban to total population in West Bengal shown in the preliminary tabulations of the 1971 Census of India[3] reflects a sharp increase in the share of urban centres other than the Calcutta urban agglomeration[4] which is only partly offset by a relative decline in the latter's share.

During each of the two decades since 1951, the growth rate of the population was considerably slower in the Calcutta urban agglomeration than in West Bengal as a whole. From 1951 to 1961, the decennial rate was 25.0 per cent for the Calcutta urban agglomeration and 32.7 per cent for West Bengal as a

---

[1] Statistical data on seasonal migration in and out of Calcutta are at present lacking. On the one hand, there is no separate tabulation of information on Calcutta in two sample surveys that have been made of internal migration in India—see *National Sample Survey*, No. 53: *Tables with notes on internal migration, 9th, 11th, 12th and 13th rounds: May 1955-May 1958* (New Delhi, Cabinet Secretariat, 1962), and *National Sample Survey*, No. 126: *Tables with notes on internal migration, 14th round: July 1958-June 1959; 15th round: July 1959-June 1960* (New Delhi, Cabinet Secretariat, 1968). On the other hand, the information on migration obtainable from the censuses of India prior to the 1971 census (see above, p. 12) deals with "lifetime migration" from place of birth to place of residence rather than with short-term movements. The 1971 census returns will tabulate occupation and migration estimates from a 20 per cent sample of the urban census slips. The tabulation will show inter-district "lifetime migration" from district of birth to district of residence and length of time since arrival at place of residence. There was no question in the census form which could yield information on intermediate stops between place of birth and current place of residence. In the case of Greater Calcutta, each of the four districts surrounding the Calcutta district (Hooghly, Howrah, 24-Parganas, Nadia) has been split into two parts which are being coded separately for the computer: *(a)* the municipalities forming part of the Calcutta urban agglomeration and *(b)* the rest of the district. This will permit tabulation of migration into and out of the Calcutta urban agglomeration as well as the city of Calcutta itself. Pending publication of these tabulations, the only available information on the migration situation in Calcutta refers to the 1951-1961 decade.

[2] Ashish Bose: "The urbanization process in South and Southeast Asia", in Leo Jakobson and Ved Prakash (ed.): *Urbanization and national development* (Beverly Hills, Sage Publications, 1971), p. 98.

[3] *Census of India, 1971*, Series 1: *India*, Paper 1 of 1971, Supplement: *Provisional population totals*, op. cit., pp. 49-50.

[4] See footnote[1], p. 3.

Table 13.   Population growth rates, West Bengal and Calcutta 1941-71

	West Bengal			Urban areas		Districts [1] in which Calcutta urban agglomeration is located	Calcutta Metropolitan District
	Total	Rural	Urban	Calcutta urban agglomeration	Other urban areas		
	(1)	(2)	(3)	(4)	(5)	(6)	(7)
Population (millions):							
1941	23.2	18.5	4.7	.	.	9.5	4.3
1951	26.3	20.0	6.3	4.6	1.7	11.5	5.4
1961	34.9	26.4	8.5	5.7	2.8	15.2	6.7
1971	44.4	33.5	10.9	7.0	3.9	19.2	8.3
Decennial growth rate (per cent):							
1941-1951	13.4	8.1	34.0	.	.	20.9	24.6
1951-1961	32.7	32.0	34.9	25.0	64.7	32.0	25.1
1961-1971	27.2	27.0	28.2	22.1	39.3	26.7	23.5

[1] Nadia, 24-Parganas, Howrah, Calcutta, Hooghly.

Sources: Cols. (1) to (5): *Census of India, 1961*, Vol. 1: *India*, Part II-A (i): *General population tables*, p. 54; *Census of India, 1971*, Series 1: *India*, Paper 1 of 1971, Supplement: *Provisional population totals*, pp. 35, 49, 50; *Statistical abstract, India, 1969*, pp. 31-32. Col. (6): *Census of India, 1971*, Series 18: *West Bengal*, Paper 1 of 1971: *Provisional population totals*, pp. 49, 51. Col. (7): for 1941-1961: Government of West Bengal, Calcutta Metropolitan Planning Organisation: *Basic development plan for the Calcutta Metropolitan District, 1966-1986*, table 5, p. 10; for 1971: idem: *A memorandum on a perspective plan for Calcutta Metropolitan District and West Bengal, 1971-1989*, p. 5.

whole, whereas from 1961 to 1971 the rates were 22.1 per cent and 27.2 per cent respectively. In the course of the latter decade, the populations of rural West Bengal and of all urban West Bengal, including Calcutta, increased by 27.0 per cent and 28.2 per cent respectively, with a resulting increase of 39.3 per cent in the population of urban West Bengal excluding the Calcutta urban agglomeration (see table 13). These growth rates, coupled with the fact that there is normally a considerable amount of migration into metropolitan Calcutta from states bordering on West Bengal and from Uttar Pradesh, imply that there was little, if any, net migration from rural West Bengal into metropolitan Calcutta.

The rate of population growth is considerably higher in the districts surrounding Calcutta than in the Calcutta urban agglomeration.[1] One of these districts, 24-Parganas, which stretches eastwards all the way to the Bangladesh border and southwards to the Bay of Bengal, is the most densely populated district in West Bengal; its decennial growth rate from 1961 to 1971 (36.6 per cent) was much higher than the average rate for all of West Bengal (27.2 per cent). In the group of five districts comprising Calcutta and the

[1] *Census of India, 1971*, Series 18: *West Bengal*, Paper 1 of 1971: *Provisional population totals*, op. cit., p. 51.

surrounding districts of Nadia, 24-Parganas, Howrah and Hooghly, the decennial growth rate was 26.7 per cent, or rather less than the average rate for all of West Bengal but considerably more than the rate of 22.1 per cent for the Calcutta urban agglomeration, which includes Calcutta itself and the contiguous urban areas in the four surrounding districts. The relatively low rate of growth of population in the urban agglomeration itself may conceal a more marked increase in the larger pool of actual or potential members of the urban labour force of metropolitan Calcutta resident in the nearby rural and non-contiguous urban areas of West Bengal.

Since the 1940s the waves of immigration which have episodically overwhelmed Calcutta have consisted not so much of migrants seeking work as of refugees fleeing from disaster. During the Second World War, refugees flooded into Calcutta because of the Bengal famine of 1943. After 1947 and again after the 1964 Indo-Pakistan war, they flooded in to escape political uncertainty and religious strife in East Pakistan. From 1946 to mid-1970, 4.2 million persons from East Pakistan registered as refugees in West Bengal, the annual influx reaching peaks of 925,000 in 1950 and 667,000 in 1964.[1] During the months leading up to the 1971 Indo-Pakistan war, between 7 and 10 million refugees poured across the border; but, following the creation of Bangladesh, most of them were quickly repatriated at the beginning of 1972.

The flood of refugees who poured into Calcutta in the 1950s was an intensification of a natural movement of persons, particularly middle-class Bengali Hindus from East Bengal[2], into what had been the capital city not only of Bengal but also, until 1912, of all India. The overwhelming seriousness of Calcutta's problems of unemployment and housing shortage in the 1950s and again in the mid-1960s was created by the accumulating numbers of displaced middle-class persons from East Pakistan arriving in Calcutta and other parts of West Bengal.

The traditional migrants from areas other than East Pakistan who came in search of employment apparently either found work of some kind or went back where they had come from. They also constituted part of the seasonal ebb and flow of the unskilled labour supply of metropolitan Calcutta. Unlike the refugees, they came without their families and could return home.

In the initial phase (1946-48) of the refugee flood, a preponderance of the refugees belonged to middle-class groups (the Bengali *bhadralok*)[3], whose level

---

[1] Bengal Chamber of Commerce and Industry: *West Bengal*, op. cit., pp. 22-23.

[2] See above, p. 16, footnote 2.

[3] See Marcus F. Franda: *Radical politics in West Bengal* (Cambridge, Mass., and London, Massachusetts Institute of Technology Press, 1971), p. 7: "Neither a single class nor a single caste, the *bhadralok* . . . are a privileged minority most often drawn from the three highest castes . . ., usually landed or employed in professional or clerical occupations . . ., very well educated . . . and highly skilled in maintaining communal integration through a complex institutional structure that has proved remarkably adaptable."

of education was higher than that of the general population of West Bengal and who had been concentrated in service occupations and in trade before migrating. Refugees from the urban areas of East Pakistan who were in the labour force had mostly been engaged in public administration and other services, while those from rural areas had mostly been occupied in trade and commerce. Persons from the border areas of East Pakistan tended to move over short distances to contiguous districts of West Bengal, while those from the interior of East Pakistan, mostly from Dacca, Faridpur and Barisal, went to the metropolitan area districts of Calcutta, 24-Parganas and Nadia.[1]

Of the early wave of refugee families, 55 per cent were high-caste and 13 per cent middle-caste.[2] Of the refugee families, 50 per cent of those coming from rural areas and 67 per cent of those from urban areas were high-caste. Of the refugees settling in "village" areas, in "town" areas and in "city" areas, 33 per cent, 60 per cent and 58 per cent respectively were high-caste.

By 1955, there were 2.2 million refugees in West Bengal.[3] This refugee population had a labour force participation rate of 36.9 per cent and an unemployed (not working but seeking work) rate of 3.9 per cent, or 10.4 per cent of its labour force. Of the labour force, 26.9 per cent were engaged in agricultural occupations, 14.6 per cent in trade, 8.2 per cent in the professions and 22.5 per cent in services.

The situation of migrants to Calcutta city in the mid-1950s is well described in the report of a sample survey carried out on behalf of the University of Calcutta by S. N. Sen for the Government of India's Planning Commission.[4] This survey revealingly broke down the Calcutta population into three groups: residents, normal migrants from other Indian states and refugees from East Pakistan. The breakdown showed that the labour force participation rates were much higher for the normal migrants (who arrived for the most part without their families) than for the resident population or for the refugees (who arrived with their families). It also showed that unemployment rates were lower for the normal migrants than for the resident population but much higher for the refugee population.

---

[1] Kanti B. Pakrasi: *The uprooted: A sociological study of the refugees of West Bengal, India* (Calcutta, Editions Indian, 1971), pp. 109, 129, 130.

[2] N. C. Chakraverti: *Report on the survey of refugee population in West Bengal (1948)* (Calcutta, 1949, mimeographed), as quoted in Pakrasi, *The uprooted*, op. cit., pp. 98-99.

[3] Government of West Bengal, State Statistical Bureau: *Rehabilitation of refugees: A statistical survey, 1955* (Calcutta, 1956), pp. 4, 7, 46, 50. This was the second of two major surveys of the refugee population carried out by the Bureau. The results of the first were published in: *Report of the sample survey for estimating the socio-economic characteristics of displaced persons migrating from Eastern Pakistan to the State of West Bengal* (Calcutta, 1951).

[4] S. N. Sen: *The city of Calcutta: A socio-economic survey, 1954-55 to 1957-58* (Calcutta, Bookland, 1960). For some particulars of the survey methods employed, see below, Annex A, pp. 101-102.

Table 14. Language pattern of Calcutta's population, 1957/58

Category	Bengali	Hindi	Urdu	Oriya	Other	Total
Sex ratio (females per 1 000 males):						
All persons	742	253	280	98	.	533
Resident population	828	441	366	240	.	.
Ordinary migrants	443	113	108	54	.	.
Displaced migrants	820	—	—	—	.	.
Distribution by sex (per cent):						
Males	54	31	.	.	.	100
Females	78	15	.	.	.	100
All persons	61	25	6	2	6	100
Distribution by age group (per cent):						
0-14	34	20	19	9	.	28
15-44	52	67	67	77	.	58
45-59	10	10	10	12	.	10
60 and over	4	3	4	2	.	4
All ages	100	100	100	100	100	100

Source: S. N. Sen: *The city of Calcutta: a socio-economic survey 1954-55 to 1957-58* (Calcutta, Bookland, 1960), pp. 16, 19, 22, 24, 25.

The language spoken is significant since it defines the geographical and, in some cases, religious origin of a Calcutta resident. Hindi speakers in Calcutta are generally Hindus from Bihar and Uttar Pradesh, Urdu speakers are generally Muslims from those same two states and Oriya speakers come from the neighbouring state of Orissa, while speakers of the less widely used Indian languages come from farther afield. In 1957/58, only 61 per cent of the inhabitants of Calcutta were Bengali-speaking, 25 per cent being Hindi-speaking, 6 per cent Urdu-speaking, 2 per cent Oriya-speaking and 1 per cent English-speaking.

The language groups differ from one another in demographic characteristics (see table 14), including especially the sex ratio. In 1957/58, the number of females per 1,000 males in the resident population of Calcutta was 828 for Bengalis, as compared with 441 for Hindi-speakers, 366 for Urdu-speakers and 240 for Oriya-speakers. The female to male ratios for ordinary migrants were much lower in all cases than for displaced migrants. Correspondingly, although only 54 per cent of Calcutta's males were Bengali-speaking, 78 per cent of the city's females were Bengali-speaking; conversely, 31 per cent of the males were Hindi-speaking but only 15 per cent of the females. The unusually high proportion of males of working age in Calcutta has its parallel in the disproportionate concentration of persons speaking Hindi, Urdu and particularly Oriya in the 15-44 age group.

It was noted in the report of the survey, though without specifying the proportions, that illiteracy among Bengali-speakers was rather high among original residents and lowest among the displaced migrants. Among the persons speaking Hindi and Urdu, illiteracy was much higher among ordinary migrants than among original residents. A statement in the report that probably still holds good was that "the city is attracting the comparatively more educated sections from among the Bengali-speaking population living outside, while among the Hindi- and Urdu-speaking people, it is the comparatively uneducated sections which have migrated to the city in large numbers".[1]

In one of the interesting tabulations presented in the survey report, ordinary migrants were classified by reported cause of migration. Except in the case of pre-Partition migrants from East Bengal, nearly one-half of whom moved for marriage and family reasons, search for employment or search for better employment were by far the most frequently cited causes.[2] The minor yet significant causes of migration included the attraction of Calcutta's educational facilities in the case of urban immigrants from West Bengal and East Pakistan and lack of land to cultivate at home in the case of rural immigrants from Bihar, Orissa and Uttar Pradesh.

In addition to absorbing the refugees from East Pakistan, West Bengal was, at the time of the 1961 census, the largest recipient of net inter-state migration in India: 2.2 million persons from other states were living in West Bengal, while 0.6 million persons born in West Bengal were living elsewhere in India, leaving a net immigration of 1.6 million.[3] Most of the immigrants came from three States, Bihar (60.6 per cent), Orissa (8.4 per cent) and Uttar Pradesh (15.6 per cent). West Bengal was the recipient of 66.6 per cent of the total flow of emigrants from Bihar, 39.9 per cent of those from Orissa and 13.5 per cent of those from Uttar Pradesh. Uttar Pradesh sent its largest contingents to Maharashtra (16.5 per cent) and Delhi (16.4 per cent).[4]

The distribution by sector of work of immigrants to West Bengal from these three states showed the highest concentrations in manufacturing and in services (see table 15). Manufacturing accounted for 16.0 per cent of the migrants from Bihar, 26.5 per cent of those from Orissa and 26.3 per cent of those from Uttar Pradesh. The proportion of non-workers was highest (40.4 per cent) among migrants from Bihar and lowest (24.6 per cent) among those from

---

[1] Sen: *The city of Calcutta*, op. cit., p. 32.

[2] Ibid., pp. 209-210.

[3] *Census of India, 1961*, Vol. I: *India*, Part II-C (iii): *Migration tables*, pp. 16, 46.

[4] Tapan Piplai and Niloy Majumdar: "Internal migration in India: Some socio-economic implications", in *Sankhyā: The Indian Journal of Statistics* (Calcutta), Series B, Vol. 31, Parts 3 and 4, Dec. 1969, pp. 518-519, quoting *Census of India, 1961*, Vol. I, Part II (A).

Table 15. Distribution of immigrants to West Bengal from Bihar, Orissa and Uttar Pradesh by sector of work, 1961

Sector of work	Bihar	Orissa	Uttar Pradesh
	(Per cent)		
Agriculture:			
Cultivators	3.5	3.0	0.5
Agricultural labourers	3.1	4.5	0.2
Mining and related [1]	8.9	7.1	3.0
Household industry	1.1	0.6	0.5
Manufacturing	16.0	26.5	26.3
Construction	2.0	2.2	1.5
Trade and commerce	7.9	7.6	10.9
Transport, storage, communication	5.2	5.4	7.0
Other services	11.9	18.5	13.3
Sub-total: workers	59.6	75.4	63.2
Non-workers	40.4	24.6	36.8
Total	100.0	100.0	100.0
Absolute numbers (thousands)	*1 351*	*187*	*347*

[1] Includes quarrying, livestock, forestry, fishing, hunting, plantation, orchards.

Sources: Tapan Piplai and Niloy Majumdar: "Internal migration in India: Some socio-economic implications", in *Sankhyā: The Indian Journal of Statistics* (Calcutta), Series B, Vol. 31, Parts 3 and 4, Dec. 1969, p. 522, quoting: *Census of India, 1961*, Vol. XVI: *West Bengal*, Part II (iii); and *Census of India, 1961*, Vol. I: *India*, Part II-C (iii): *Migration tables*, p. 46.

Orissa, the latter having come without their families to an even greater extent than other migrants.

An analysis made by K. R. Chakraverty of the situation of migrants to Calcutta city as revealed by the 1961 census shows that in 1961, 53 per cent of the city's enumerated population had been born outside the city. Of the 1.5 million immigrants, 34 per cent came from East Pakistan, 20 per cent from other districts of West Bengal, 22 per cent from Bihar, 4 per cent from Orissa, less than 1 per cent from Assam and the rest from elsewhere. Over half of the migrants from West Bengal, however, came from the districts adjoining Calcutta—24-Parganas, Howrah, Hooghly and Nadia.[1] Labour force participation rates were considerably higher among migrants than among the resident population, except for males in the 35-59 age group (see table 16). The distribution of the working population by economic sector showed a somewhat lower proportion of the migrants than of the resident population in manufacturing but a higher proportion in trade and in other services, though with some variation by state of origin (see table 17).

---

[1] K. R. Chakraverty: *A study of the life-time in-migration to Calcutta city*, Ph.D. dissertation, University of Pennsylvania, Department of Demography (1967, typescript), p. 12.

Table 16. Work force participation rates for resident immigrants and non-immigrants by sex and age, Calcutta city, 1961
(Per cent)

Age group	Males		Females	
	Non-immigrants	Immigrants	Non-immigrants	Immigrants
0-14	—	4.2	—	0.4
15-34	67.0	80.6	4.8	9.3
35-59	99.0	89.9	12.2	17.1
60+	47.7	54.6	5.8	5.8

Source: K. R. Chakraverty: *A study of the life-time in-migration to Calcutta city*, Ph.D. dissertation, University of Pennsylvania, Department of Demography (1967, typescript), p. 36, quoting *Census of India, 1961*, Vol. XVI, Part II-C (iii), Table D IV, and Part II-B (iii).

Table 17. Distribution of male non-immigrant and immigrant population by selected geographical origin and by sector of activity, Calcutta city, 1961
(Per cent)

Sector	Non-immigrants	Immigrants from:				
		All sources	West Bengal	Bihar	Orissa	East Pakistan
Agriculture, mining	0.2	0.3	0.3	0.3	1.0	0.2
Household industry	0.5	0.8	0.6	1.6	0.3	0.6
Manufacturing	29.3	25.0	30.2	22.4	22.0	27.1
Construction	3.1	3.5	4.9	4.3	4.4	2.3
Trade and commerce	24.6	25.1	21.2	25.3	18.3	24.3
Transport	11.6	12.5	11.2	15.4	12.2	10.2
Other services	30.7	32.8	31.6	30.7	41.8	35.3
Total	100.0	100.0	100.0	100.0	100.0	100.0

Source: Chakraverty: *A study of the life-time in-migration to Calcutta city*, op. cit., pp. 39, 40, quoting *Census of India, 1961*, Vol. XVI, Part II-C (iii), Table D VI, and Part II-A.

In India's Eastern Region, which is Calcutta's hinterland, migration to metropolitan Calcutta is, for most people, probably due more to a lack of employment opportunities in their places of origin than simply to the prospect of higher earnings in the big city that would result from higher unit rates of pay: for an employed unskilled worker, unit rates of pay may not be much better in the big city than in his place of origin. Although the statutory minimum daily wage for an agricultural labourer in West Bengal in 1972 was about Rs 3.75 including meals, in practice the wage rate paid in the poorer districts of the western part of West Bengal never exceeded Rs 2.70 at the peak seasons (six to eight weeks of the year) and ranged between Rs 1.50 and Rs 2 per day during the rest of the year.[1] In Burdwan, on the other hand, peak season wage rates for agricultural labourers exceeded the statutory minimum wage. In Calcutta, in December 1971, the statutory minimum wage of an unskilled worker under the Minimum Wages Act was as low as Rs 50.44 per month in rice milling and Rs 52 per month in stone breaking and in construction and road building.[2] The highest rates are paid in the engineering industry, which is one of the major branches (the others being jute and textiles) for which tripartite (labour, management and government) wage agreements have fixed industry-wide minimum wages. In general, the industry-wide wage agreements also apply to small units, though at a lower scale of remuneration than for large units. Nevertheless, some of the new small firms starting up in the engineering sector will pay to new hands, who are regarded as apprentices, as little as Rs 75-100 per month although the minimum wage negotiated for unskilled labour which was effective early in 1972 was Rs 178 per month in plants employing 50-249 workers. For the unskilled, therefore, the incentive to move into the city is probably not so much the difference in wage rate as the greater probability of finding some employment in the larger market created by the big city than in the village, where there is a clear excess of labour in agriculture except at the peak seasons. The imminent modernisation of agriculture in West Bengal and eventually in Bihar[3] could transform this situation both by raising productivity and incomes in agriculture and by increasing the number of seasonal peaks in agriculture through irrigation and multiple cropping.

For the educated in rural areas of West Bengal, the outlook is even clearer. Until modernised agriculture creates manpower demands in the small towns servicing an expanding agricultural sector, there will be few employment possibilities for them except in the big city.

How do people find employment in metropolitan Calcutta? Most of the studies[4] show that the largest proportion of job-seekers find work through friends and relatives, through fellow villagers or townsmen and through caste affiliations. New arrivals seeking factory employment will often stay with an already employed relative and then try to obtain a temporary job at the same place of work, usually as casual labourers who will then gain some skill on

---

[1] D. Bandyopadhyay, Labour Commissioner, West Bengal: *The rate of wages of agricultural workers: A case study of two Bankura villages* (Calcutta, 1972), p. 10.

[2] Government of West Bengal, Labour Directorate, Statistics, Research and Publication Branch: *Labour in West Bengal, 1971* (Calcutta, 1972), p. 34.

[3] See below, Chapter 5.

[4] See, in particular, Sen: *The city of Calcutta*, op. cit., pp. 76-78, and Reserve Bank of India: *Survey of small engineering units in Howrah*, Report of a survey undertaken by Jadavpur University (Calcutta and Bombay, 1964), pp. 36, 89.

Table 18. Non-agricultural working population, West Bengal, 1961, 1971
('000)

Category	Rural	Urban	Total
Total population			
1961	2 444	2 906	5 350
1971	2 184	3 174	5 358
Males			
1961	1 972	2 730	4 702
1971	1 847	2 962	4 809
Females			
1961	472	176	648
1971	337	212	549

Source: *Census of India, 1971*, Series 1: *India*, Paper 1 of 1971, Supplement: *Provisional population totals*, op. cit., pp. 60-73.

the job. In recent years, one of the main activities of the trade unions has been to apply pressure on the factories to recruit permanent staff from among the temporary casual labourers already on the job.

WORKING POPULATION AND EMPLOYMENT

According to the provisional results of the 1971 Census of India, the total non-agricultural working population in West Bengal was almost the same in 1971 as it had been in 1961. This was partly due to the fact that persons engaged in family economic activity on a less than full-time basis were classified in the 1971 Census as non-workers. As a result of this change in definition, the absolute number of female non-agricultural workers reported in the 1971 Census showed a decline of about 100,000, which offset an increase of about 100,000 in the absolute number of male non-agricultural workers (see table 18). Over the decade, the number of rural non-agricultural workers fell by about 11 per cent, while the number of urban non-agricultural workers rose by about 9 per cent, with the arithmetical result of a net shift of 260,000 non-agricultural workers from rural to urban areas of West Bengal. The shift occurred for both males and females, although in the case of females the apparent shift may have resulted only from a reduction in the number of working women in rural households owing to the change in definition.

The non-agricultural working population of West Bengal in 1969 may be estimated at around 5.3 million persons, of whom 2.2 million were in rural and 3.1 million in urban areas (see table 19). In that year, the official statistics on non-agricultural employment in registered activities covered only 2.1 million

Table 19. Employment in non-agricultural registered establishments, West Bengal, 1961, 1965-70 ('000)

Sector	1961	1965	1966	1967	1968	1969	1970
1. Coal mines	125	122	118	118	111	109	110
2. Manufacturing: registered factories [1]	.	910	840	865	850	791	809
3. Electricity:							
a. State Electricity Board	.	.	16	15	15	15	16
b. Calcutta Electricity Supply Corporation	.	.	10	10	10	10	10
4. Transport:							
a. Calcutta Tramways	.	.	10	10	10	10	11
b. Calcutta State Transport	.	.	14	14	14	13	13
c. Calcutta Port [2]	.	.	61	62	61	58	.
5. Trade and services:							
a. Shops	.	.	169	177	189	199	.
b. Commercial establishments	.	.	97	102	115	120	.
c. Hotels and restaurants	.	.	44	49	53	55	.
d. Cinemas and theatres	.	.	5	4	5	6	.
6. Government offices:							
a. State Government	211	250	255	263	268	279	280
b. Central Government	.	.	415	416	424	418	410
c. Calcutta Corporation	.	.	30	30	28	28	.
d. Howrah Municipality	.	.	5	5	5	5	.
Total [1]	.	.	2 099	2 140	2 158	2 116	.

[1] Registered small-scale industry units, which form only a small part of the total household manufacturing sector, are not included in this table. Employment in the registered units amounted (in '000) to: 1966:18; 1967:19; 1968:30; 1969:34; 1970:45. ² Port Commissioners, seamen, dock labour.

Sources: Line 1: 1966-70: Government of West Bengal: *Economic review, year 1971-72*, op. cit., p. 98; 1961, 1965: Government of West Bengal, State Statistical Bureau: *Statistical handbook, 1966*, p. 87. Lines 2, 3, 4, 5, 6.c, 6.d: 1965-70: Government of West Bengal, Labour Directorate, Statistics Branch: *Handbook of labour statistics, West Bengal, 1970*, pp. 4-7, 101-105; 1961: comparable figures not available; 1970 figure for line 2 taken from Government of West Bengal: *Economic review, year 1971-72*, op. cit., p. 98. Lines 6.a. 6.b: 1961, 1967-70: Government of West Bengal: *Economic review, year 1969-70*, p. 83. Footnote 1: Government of West Bengal: *Economic review, year 1971-72*, op. cit., p. 96.

Table 20. Employment in non-agricultural registered establishments, metropolitan Calcutta, 1961, 1965-71 ('000)

Sector	1961	1965	1966	1967	1968	1969	1970	1971
1. Coal mines	.	.	.	.	.	.	.	.
2. Manufacturing: Registered factories[1]	600	739	698	696	672	641	652	654
3. Electricity:								
a. State Electricity Board	.	.	.	.	.	.	.	.
b. Calcutta Electricity Supply Corporation				10	10	10	10	
4. Transport:								
a. Calcutta Tramways			10	10	10	10	11	
b. Calcutta State Transport			14	14	14	13	13	
c. Calcutta Port			61	62	61	58		
5. Trade and services[2]:								
a. Shops			124	131	136	144	149	
b. Commercial establishments			82	98	101	104	107	
c. Hotels and restaurants			34	38	41	42	43	
d. Cinemas and theatres			3	3	3	3	3	
6. Government offices:								
a. State Government						130		
b. Central Government						270[3]		
c. Calcutta Corporation			30	30	28	28		
d. Howrah Municipality			5	5	5	5		

[1] Calcutta, Howrah, 24-Parganas and Hooghly districts. Registered establishments, which form only a small part of the total household manufacturing sector, are not included in this table. Employment in the registered units amounted (in '000) to: 1966 : 9; 1967 : 13; 1968 : 24; 1969 : 24; 1970 : 31. [2] Calcutta City. [3] Assumed to be 65 per cent of figure for West Bengal.

Sources: Line 2: A. N. Bose: *A note on the economic development programme for the Calcutta Metropolitan District* (Calcutta, Calcutta Metropolitan Planning Organisation, 1972), p. 8. Lines 3.b, 4, 5, 6.c, 6.d: Government of West Bengal, Labour Directorate, Statistical Branch: *Handbook of labour statistics, West Bengal, 1970*, pp. 101-105. Line 6.a: Government of West Bengal, State Planning Board. Footnote 1: Government of West Bengal: *Economic review, year 1971-72*, op. cit., p. 96.

persons: 0.9 million in mining and manufacturing, over 0.7 million in central, state and local government offices and 0.5 million in transport, trade and some services.

Assuming Calcutta's share of West Bengal's urban working population to be the same as its share of West Bengal's total urban population[1], it may be estimated that in 1969 about 2.1 million of West Bengal's urban working population were in the Calcutta urban agglomeration. Of the jobs covered by the official employment statistics, perhaps 1.5 million were in the Calcutta Metropolitan District, assuming that 65 per cent of the employees of the Government of India in West Bengal were located in metropolitan Calcutta (see table 20).

The official employment statistics thus cover at most about two-thirds of the urban working population both in West Bengal as a whole and in metropolitan Calcutta. There is some overlap, however, between registered activities and the informal sector.[2] For example, most of the plethora of smaller establishments covered by the Shops and Establishments Act are family enterprises whose activities lie outside the modern, organised part of the economy. This is true also of the registered small-scale industry units shown in footnotes to tables 19 and 20. In these tables, the number of registered small-scale industry units apparently covers such a small portion of the household manufacturing sector that it may be considered less misleading to exclude them entirely from the statistics on the registered sector than to include them. The entire household manufacturing sector forms part of the informal sector.

Pending availability of all the 1971 Census tabulations, it is useful to re-examine some of the results of several labour force surveys carried out in Calcutta in the 1950s. Each of them gives some idea of the sectoral and occupational structure of Calcutta's working population. Unfortunately, the classifications used vary considerably from survey to survey, making it impossible to deduce any time trends from the survey materials. They all serve, however, to emphasise the large proportion of all activities that falls outside the organised sectors of manufacturing, financial and business services and government.

The first of these surveys was carried out in 1953 by the Indian Statistical Institute.[3] This survey of employment in Calcutta presented a fairly detailed breakdown of the gainfully employed by economic sector and by occupation.

---

[1] *Census of India, 1971*, Series 1: *India*, Paper 1 of 1971, Supplement: *Provisional population totals*, op. cit., pp. 49-50.

[2] On the concept of the informal sector see ILO: *Employment, incomes and equality: A strategy for increasing productive employment in Kenya* (Geneva, 1972), Ch. 13.

[3] *National Sample Survey*, No. 17: *Report on sample survey of employment in Calcutta, 1953* (Delhi, Cabinet Secretariat, 1959). For some particulars of the survey methods employed, see below, Annex A, p. 101.

The breakdown by sector showed 25 per cent in distribution and finance, 26 per cent in manufacturing, 30 per cent in services and the rest in construction, public utilities and other activities (see table 21). The breakdown by occupation showed 38 per cent in white-collar jobs (administrative and executive, ministerial, and superior technical occupations), 15 per cent in trade and financial occupations, 29 per cent in skilled manual occupations and 18 per cent in unskilled occupations (see table 22).

From a survey of Calcutta covering the years 1955/56 to 1957/58 to which reference has already been made[1], S. N. Sen estimates as follows the distribution of earners in Calcutta city by economic sector: 38 per cent in distribution, 16 per cent in manufacturing, 24 per cent in services and the rest in construction, public utilities and other activities. The distribution by occupational group showed 21 per cent in white-collar jobs (executive, technical and professional, ministerial), 18 per cent in skilled manual jobs, 34 per cent in unskilled manual jobs and 24 per cent in trade occupations. In both distributions, unearned incomes supported 2 per cent of the income recipients.[2]

A more detailed occupational breakdown, which can be pieced together from Sen's discussion (see table 23), shows that 3.5 per cent of the skilled manual workers were occupied in the building trades (builders, plumbers, masons, carpenters) and 4.8 per cent in the engineering trades (turners, grinders, drillers, moulders, smelters, smiths), only 2.8 per cent of them falling into a category called "factory workers", and that one-third of the working population consisted of unskilled manual workers carrying out all those low-productivity tasks that keep the city moving, eating and as clean as it ever is—cooks, domestic servants, watchmen, peons, bearers, sweepers and scavengers, rickshaw pullers, porters, washermen, gardeners, waste paper collectors, etc. Most of these unskilled manual workers form part of the informal sector.

According to a survey of Calcutta and the surrounding industrial areas carried out in 1959 by the State Statistical Bureau[3], and which used a somewhat different set of occupational groupings, earners in Calcutta alone (excluding the surrounding areas) were distributed as follows: 30 per cent in white-collar occupations (professional, technical, owners, managers, officials and clerical employees) and 35 per cent in trade and services occupations, the remaining 35 per cent being skilled and unskilled manual workers (including unreported) (see table 24). In Calcutta and the surrounding industrial areas, the shares were, as would be expected, lower for white-collar occupations (24.4 per cent)

---

[1] See above, p. 37.

[2] Sen: *The city of Calcutta*, op. cit., pp. 63, 66.

[3] Government of West Bengal, State Statistical Bureau: *Report on the survey of unemployment in Calcutta and Calcutta industrial areas, 1959* (Calcutta, 1966).

Table 21. Distribution of gainfully employed persons in Calcutta city by economic sector, 1953

	Per cent
Agriculture and related; mining and quarrying	*1.2*
Construction	*2.6*
Manufacturing	*26.0*
Food, drink, tobacco	4.4
Cotton, jute, woollen textiles and products	2.5
Wood, paper, leather, and products	4.3
Chemicals	2.1
Metal and machinery	7.4
Printing	3.1
Other manufacturing	2.2
Distributive trades and financial operations	*25.4*
Wholesale trade	6.8
Retail trade	15.7
Import, export and financial operations	2.9
Transport, communications and public utilities	*15.2*
Transport	11.8
Communications	2.1
Electricity, gas, water, sanitary services	1.3
Services	*29.6*
Public services	5.5
Educational services	1.8
Medical and health services	2.1
Domestic and personal services	13.9
Other services	6.3
Total	**100.0**

Source: *National Sample Survey*, No. 17: *Report on sample survey of employment in Calcutta, 1953* (Delhi, Cabinet Secretariat, 1959), pp. 43, 45.

and for sales and services occupations (28.4 per cent) and much higher for manual workers (47.2 per cent).

In the same survey's detailed occupational breakdown for Calcutta city, skilled manual workers (handicraftsmen, operatives, and skilled labour in manufacturing) accounted for 23 per cent of all earners and unskilled (including occupations not reported) for 12 per cent. In the Calcutta industrial area as a whole, the shares were 31.3 per cent for skilled manual workers and 15.9 per cent for unskilled (including occupations not reported).[1]

According to the 1961 population Census, 20 per cent of the working population (other than cultivators) of urban West Bengal were occupied in trade and commerce, 34 per cent in manufacturing (other than household industry), 29 per cent in services and the rest in construction, transport and

---

[1] For fuller particulars, see below, Annex A, table 42.

Table 22. Distribution of gainfully employed persons in Calcutta city by occupational group, 1953

	Per cent
Superior administrative and executive	*3.4*
Subordinate administrative and executive	*16.5*
Management and supervision	2.9
Other	13.6
Ministerial	*11.7*
Distributive services and financial operations	*14.7*
Superior technical	*6.3*
Engineering, technology, scientific research	1.1
Medical and health	1.0
Teaching and training	1.4
Literature, art, etc.	0.7
Law	0.9
Other	1.2
Skilled artisans, craftsmen, operators, workers	*28.8*
General engineering	0.5
Building industry	1.5
Manufacture of food, beverages, intoxicants, oils	2.2
Printing industry	1.8
Medical	0.6
Tailors, barbers, laundrymen, cooks, etc.	7.4
Other	14.8
Unskilled workers, and others unspecified	*18.6*
Total	**100.0**

Source: as for table 21.

other activities (see table 25). The breakdown by occupation group showed 21 per cent in white-collar jobs (professional, administrative and clerical), 30 per cent in trade and service occupations and 49 per cent in manual occupations. In the Calcutta industrial area, as defined by the 1961 Census, 19 per cent of the working population other than cultivators were in distribution, 39 per cent in manufacturing other than household industry, 27 per cent in services and the rest in construction, transport and other activities. [1]

---

[1] Up-to-date estimates of the working population of urban West Bengal and of the Calcutta urban agglomeration will become available once tabulations of the 1971 population census material are completed. Although the definitions of working population in the 1961 and 1971 Censuses raise some problems of comparability, the difficulties relate mainly to the status of rural households and should be much less acute in the case of the urban population. For discussions of the comparability problem, see *Census of India, 1971*, Series 1: *India*, Paper 1 of 1971, Supplement: *Provisional population totals* (New Delhi, 1971), Chapter III, pp. 23-34; and Pravin Visaria: "The provisional 1971 census data on the size and composition of the working force", in *Times of India*, 9 July 1971.

Table 23. Distribution of earners in Calcutta city by occupation, 1955/56-1957/58

Occupation	Weighted average of 3 years (per cent)
Non-technical executive: higher.	*1.5*
Managers, directors, managing agents, secretaries	0.8
Magistrates, police superintendents, commissioners, high officials of private firms, heads of departments	0.7
Non-technical executive: lower	*2.1*
Technical and professional: higher	*2.6*
Accountants, auditors, barristers, advocates, solicitors, engineers, pilot officers, medical practitioners, college and university teachers, artists, painters, musicians, photographers	2.6
Technical and professional: lower.	*3.2*
Compounders, vaccinators.	0.8
Non-qualified medical practitioners, nurses, school teachers, *muktears* and *peshkars* (municipal court officials), bailiffs, surveyors, draughtsmen, contractors	2.4
Ministerial: technical	*2.7*
Typists, stenographers.	1.3
Accounts clerks, telephone operators, telephonists.	1.4
Ministerial: non-technical	*8.7*
Clerks, assistants.	8.2
Cashiers, time keepers.	0.5
Skilled manual.	*18.5*
Builders, plumbers, masons, carpenters	3.5
Turners, grinders, drillers, moulders, smelters, smiths	4.8
Drivers, potters, engineers, jewellers, watchmakers, bookbinders, radio mechanics, electricians.	5.3
Tailors	2.1
Factory workers	2.8
Unskilled manual.	*33.7*
Cooks, domestic servants	8.8
Darwans (watchmen), peons, bearers	7.6
Sweepers and scavengers.	1.3
Rickshaw pullers, handcart pullers, and drivers.	4.0
Porters	7.3
Washermen, cobblers, barbers	4.4
Malis (gardeners), waste paper collectors, *biri* (cigarette) makers	0.3
Traders.	*23.5*
Retail proprietors.	9.0
Shop assistants, salesmen	5.4
Brokers and auctioneers	2.0
Wholesale proprietors, canvassers, commercial agents	3.5
Street hawkers	3.6
Unearned income receivers.	*2.1*
Miscellaneous	*1.4*
Beggars, prostitutes, persons of questionable livelihood	1.4
Total	**100.0**

Source: Sen: *The city of Calcutta*, op. cit., pp. 65-69.

Table 24. Distribution of earners by occupation group, Calcutta [1] and surrounding industrial areas [2], 1959

Occupation group	Number ('000)		Per cent			Bengalis as per cent of all earners	
	Calcutta [1]	Calcutta and industrial areas [2]	Calcutta [1]	Calcutta and industrial areas [2]		Calcutta [1]	Calcutta and industrial areas [2]
Professional, technical and related	105.7	157.1	8.7	7.3		80.0	81.0
Owners, tenants, managers, officials (agriculture and related)	2.6	5.0	0.2	0.2		69.5	79.9
Owners, managers, officials (non-agricultural, non-technical)	57.7	73.9	4.8	3.5		61.3	64.2
Clerical and related	197.4	287.8	16.3	13.4		75.4	78.4
Sales workers	210.7	313.7	17.4	14.7		59.6	50.7
Handicraftsmen (mainly manual)	160.0	271.2	13.2	12.7		60.5	56.1
Operatives (mainly mechanised)	29.3	44.6	2.4	2.1		36.6	38.7
Services	213.9	294.2	17.6	13.7		39.8	39.6
Labour	231.5	688.7	19.1	32.2		31.7	27.2
Not reported	3.6	4.7	0.3	0.2		81.1	87.2
Total	1 212.4	2 140.9	100.0	100.0		53.4	48.7

[1] City, including Tollygunge. [2] The industrial areas are defined as comprising most of the contiguous and predominantly built-up municipalities within the Calcutta Metropolitan District, i.e. all except Baruipur, Rajpur and Budge-Budge in the south, Barasat in the east and Bansberia in the north. Asansol, which is about 175 km north-west of Calcutta in the Damodar Valley, is also included.

Source: Government of West Bengal, State Statistical Bureau: *Report on the survey of unemployment in Calcutta and Calcutta industrial areas, 1959* (Calcutta, 1966), pp. 18-19.

Table 25. Distribution of persons at work (other than cultivators) by economic sector and by occupation group in urban West Bengal and Calcutta industrial region according to 1961 population census

Category	Number ('000)		Per cent	
	Urban West Bengal	Calcutta industrial region	Urban West Bengal	Calcutta industrial region
Total persons at work (other than cultivators)	2 906	2 416	100.0	100.0
By economic sector:				
Mining, quarrying and activities related to agriculture	29	13	1.0	0.6
Household industry	67	37	2.3	1.5
Manufacturing (other than household industry)	983	933	33.8	38.6
Construction	92	69	3.2	2.9
Trade and commerce	583	468	20.1	19.4
Transport, storage and communications	304	235	10.5	9.7
Other services	848	661	29.2	27.3
By occupational group:				
Professional, technical and related workers	173	.	5.9	.
Administrative, executive and managerial workers	106	.	3.6	.
Clerical and related workers	345	.	11.9	.
Sales workers	479	.	16.5	.
Farmers, fishermen, hunters, loggers and related	27	.	0.9	.
Miners, quarrymen and related workers	4	.	0.1	.
Transport and communication occupations	151	.	5.2	.
Craftsmen, production process workers and labourers, n.e.c.	1 211	.	41.7	.
Service, sport and recreation workers	386	.	13.3	.
Workers not classifiable by occupation	26	.	0.9	.

Source: *Census of India, 1961*, Vol. I: *India*, Part II-B (ii): *General economic tables* (New Delhi, 1966), pp. 525-552, and Part II-A (ii): *Union primary census abstracts*, pp. 168-171.

ESTIMATES OF UNEMPLOYMENT

A major difficulty to be faced in discussing unemployment and under-employment in Calcutta lies in the choice of a meaningful and consistent set of definitions.[1] The following discussion is focused on the simple concept of open unemployment as providing the clearest indicator of the magnitude of Calcutta's employment problem. Even this concept can be, however, an equivocal one because the time dimension of "employment" is variously defined from one survey to another: the reference period may be the day, the week or the month of the enquiry and the minimum time in respect of which a person is counted as an employed member of the labour force may be one or more days within the reference period or a certain number of hours within the day.[2]

The broader concept of underemployment is even more difficult to apply in practice inasmuch as it involves consideration of at least three questions: time spent, productivity in terms of income received, and the quality, as well as the status, of the activity in relation to the physical and mental skills of the worker. Of these three aspects of underemployment, time spent is the easiest one to assess and is the only one considered in the present study. It is, however, meaningful only if the person is engaged in paid employment and not if the worker is self-employed: in the case of the self-employed, it is the income aspect of underemployment that is potentially meaningful, though the level of poverty below which an earner is to be defined as underemployed will differ from one society to another. As for the question of the quality of the activity, this aspect of underemployment might be regarded as relevant in the case of a rich and economically developed country.[3] It is, however, applicable also in the case of a less developed country in so far as a worker's reluctance to take a job below his qualifications or desired status transforms potential underemployment into actual open unemployment.

The sources of information on unemployment in Calcutta are of two kinds—namely, sample surveys of households and the registration rolls of the employment exchanges of the National Employment Service. The data which these sources provide are examined in the next two sub-sections of this chapter.

---

[1] There are numerous publications on this general subject. See for example Jean Mouly: "Some remarks on the concepts of employment, underemployment and unemployment", in *International Labour Review* (Geneva, ILO), Vol. 105, No. 2, Feb. 1972, pp. 155-160; ILO: *Concepts of labour force utilisation* (Geneva, ILO, 1971); idem: "Measuring the adequacy of employment in developing countries", in *Journal of Development Planning*, 1972, No. 5, pp. 145-164. In India, what is now the classic statement of the definitional problem is contained in the Dantwala Committee's *Report of the committee of experts on unemployment estimates* (Government of India, Planning Commission, 1970).

[2] For particulars of the reference periods used in the various surveys of employment and unemployment in Calcutta, see below, Annex A.

[3] In France, for example, the term "underemployment" is used primarily in the sense of working below one's qualitative capacity.

Household survey data

There have been three sample surveys of unemployment specifically concerned with Calcutta.[1] All of them were carried out during the 1950s[2] and have already been mentioned. The first was the Indian Statistical Institute's 1953 sample survey of employment in Calcutta.[3] The second was the enquiry, likewise focused on employment and unemployment, carried out by the University of Calcutta over the three-year period 1955/56-1957/58.[4] The third was the West Bengal State Statistical Bureau's 1959 survey of unemployment in Calcutta and the surrounding industrial areas.[5]

These three studies reveal a fairly consistent general pattern.[6] They show that, in the 1950s, the population of Calcutta city had an abnormal sex ratio of only 600-700 females to 1,000 males, indicating that a sizeable proportion of the male labour force had left their wives and families "at home" somewhere else. The over-all labour force participation rate was high (about 40 per cent), partly because of the large proportion of males in the total population. There was a labour force participation rate of over 60 per cent for Calcutta's males but of considerably less than 10 per cent for Calcutta's females. Well over 50 per cent of Calcutta city's labour force were migrants from outside of West Bengal, with over 25 per cent coming as normal migrants from other states in India and close to 20 per cent as refugees from East Pakistan. Most of the migrants from other Indian states arrived with a low level of education (over one-third of them were illiterate) and took up employment as unskilled manual workers, whereas among the migrants from East Pakistan there was a heavy concentration of educated persons who sought jobs in trade and services. As a result of the large proportion of refugees from East Pakistan in the total number of migrants, the general level of education was higher in the migrant group as a whole than among the original residents of Calcutta.

Unemployment rates were low for ordinary migrants, quite high for original residents and extremely high (over 35 per cent) for displaced migrants from East Pakistan. Correspondingly, unemployment rates were low for illiterate unskilled manual workers and high for literate and educated non-manual workers, so that the situation of the educated unemployed in Calcutta

---

[1] There have also been a number of all-India sample surveys of employment and unemployment. The samples were, however, considered too small to provide separate data on Calcutta. For some particulars of those all-India surveys, see below, Annex A, pp. 105.

[2] The results of an unemployment survey carried out in 1963 by the West Bengal State Statistical Bureau have not been released.

[3] See above, p. 46, and tables 21 and 22.

[4] Sen: *The city of Calcutta*, op. cit.; see above, pp. 37, 42, 47.

[5] See above, p. 47, and table 24.

[6] They are more fully described below in Annex A.

was already one of crisis in the 1950s. The highest unemployment rates affected the younger age groups, 16-20 and 21-25.

Unemployment rates were variously estimated as follows:

Area and year	% of labour force
Calcutta city, excluding Tollygunge[1]:	
1953[2]	18.0
1954/55[3]	10.0
1955/56[3]	9.2
1956/57[3]	7.6
Calcutta city, including Tollygunge[1]:	
1959[4]	11.8
Calcutta city, including Tollygunge[1] and surrounding industrial areas[5], including Asansol:	
1959[4]	12.0

[1] The former Tollygunge municipal area was incorporated into the Calcutta municipal area in 1953. However, the scope of a number of statistical surveys and series was not adjusted until some years later.   [2] Indian Statistical Institute.   [3] Calcutta University.   [4] West Bengal State Statistical Bureau.   [5] The definition of these areas is given in footnote 2 to table 24 (p. 51 above).

Two of these three studies also showed the number of days worked by those recorded as employed—data that can be used to give an indication of the time dimension of underemployment. In the sample covered by the Indian Statistical Institute 1953 survey, 6.3 per cent of persons employed ("gainfully occupied") on the day of the inquiry had worked on fewer than 20 out of the 30 preceding days. On the other hand, in the sample covered by the State Statistical Bureau study of 1959, less than 1 per cent of employed persons, i.e. those working full-time on at least one day of the week preceding the inquiry, had worked on only four days or less during that week.

As for the 1960s, although annual national sample surveys were carried out in those years as well as in the 1950s, the data on labour force which they provide do not deal separately with Calcutta. From the ninth round (May-November 1955) to the fifteenth round (July 1959-June 1960), Calcutta is combined in the survey reports with India's three other big cities (Bombay, Delhi and Madras) as one urban stratum. From the seventeenth round (September 1961-July 1962) onwards, Calcutta is combined with the rest of urban West Bengal. There is thus no available survey information on unemployment in Calcutta during the 1960s.

There has, however, been a recent unemployment survey covering all of West Bengal. It was carried out in 1971 by the Government of West Bengal's Bureau of Applied Economics and Statistics.[1] A preliminary global figure puts

[1] Government of West Bengal, Bureau of Applied Economics and Statistics: *A preliminary report on unemployment survey, 1971, in West Bengal* (Calcutta, 1972).

Table 26.   Population, labour force, employment and unemployment in West Bengal, 1963 and 1971

Item	1963	1971
Absolute numbers in thousands:		
Employed (full time employment at least one day in the week preceding the enquiry)	10 399	12 188
Unemployed (no full time employment on any day of week preceding the enquiry)	469	693
Labour force	10 868	12 881
Total population	37 856	44 440
Percentage of total population		
Employed	27.47	27.42
Unemployed	1.24	1.56
In labour force	28.71	28.98
Percentage of labour force		
Employed	95.7	94.6
Unemployed	4.3	5.4

Source: Government of West Bengal, Bureau of Applied Economics and Statistics: *A preliminary report on unemployment survey, 1971, in West Bengal* (Calcutta, 1972), p. 3.

the total number of unemployed in West Bengal[1] at an estimated 690,000, an unemployed person being defined as one who had had no full-time employment on any day of the week preceding the date of the enquiry and who was either looking for or available for full-time employment. This figure corresponded to 1.56 per cent of the total population of West Bengal, or 5.4 per cent of the labour force (see table 26). An additional 2 million persons seeking or available for work had been employed full-time on less than half the days of the week preceding the enquiry. This figure of 2 million provides one estimate of the underemployed according to what is essentially a definition of the time dimension of underemployment. (The sampling frame used in the survey for urban areas distinguished Calcutta and the Calcutta industrial area from other municipal towns; but estimates for these categories had not yet been released at the time of completion of the present study.)

Employment exchange registrations

The number of applicants on the live register at the employment exchanges of the National Employment Service in West Bengal fell from 457,000 in

---

[1] Separate data for urban West Bengal or for Calcutta and the surrounding industrial areas had not yet been released at the time of completion of the present study.

Table 27.   Employment exchange applicants on live register at end of year, by level of education and area of registration, West Bengal, 1966-1971

Year	Absolute numbers ('000)					Per cent	
	Total	Level of education		Area of registration		Educated as % of total West Bengal (2)÷(1)	Metropolitan Calcutta as % of West Bengal (4)÷(1)
		Educated [1]	Not educated	Metropolitan Calcutta [2]	Other West Bengal		
	(1)	(2)	(3)	(4)	(5)	(6)	(7)
1966	457	136	321	301	156	29.8	65.9
1967	446	141	305	295	151	31.6	66.1
1968	445	158	287	298	147	35.5	67.0
1969	500	183	317	336	164	36.6	67.2
1970	586	226	360	381	205	38.6	65.0
1971	867	.	.	508	359	.	58.6

[1] School Final level and higher.   [2] Includes the following offices: Central Calcutta, Kidderpore, Howrah, Barrackpore, North Calcutta, South Calcutta, Serampore, Chinsura, Kalyani, Dum Dum, East Calcutta, Calcutta and Jadavpur Universities, Special Cell Employment Bureau and Professional and Executive Cells.

Source: 1966-1970: Government of West Bengal, Labour Directorate, Statistics Branch: *Handbook of labour statistics, West Bengal, 1970* (Calcutta, 1971), pp. 13, 14.   1971: data kindly supplied by A. R. Sen Gupta, Employment Officer, Directorate of National Employment Service, West Bengal.

December 1966 to 445,000 in December 1968, but thereafter rose rapidly and at an accelerating rate, reaching 586,000 in December 1970 and soaring to 867,000 in December 1971 (see table 27). The proportion of educated persons (School Final level and higher) among them rose steadily from 29.8 per cent in 1966 to 38.6 per cent in 1970. The number of applicants registered in the exchanges located within the Calcutta Metropolitan District, as a proportion of all applicants, rose slightly from 65.9 per cent in 1966 to 67.2 per cent in 1969 but then fell off sharply in the next two years, dropping to 58.6 per cent in 1971. From 1970 to 1971, the total number of persons on the live register rose by 48 per cent in all of West Bengal and by 33 per cent in the Calcutta Metropolitan District, where it reached 508,000 by the end of 1971. Outside metropolitan Calcutta, the number rose in 1971 by 75 per cent to 359,000.

The number of registrants cannot ordinarily be used as a direct measure of the number of unemployed: on the one hand, not all the unemployed register and, on the other hand, some of those registered are already employed but are looking for better jobs. The number of registrants will equal the actual number of unemployed only if the proportion of unemployed who are registered happens to equal the proportion of registrants who are effectively unemployed (that is, who are not already employed elsewhere). Moreover, the proportions of unemployed who are registered and of registrants who are already employed probably change from year to year. It is most unlikely that an increase in the number on the live register as large as the one that occurred in 1971 reflected

Table 28. Number of urban unemployed at end of year in West Bengal as estimated from employment exchange data, 1969-1971

('000)

Category	1969	1970	1971
1. Persons on employment exchange live register	500	600	900
2. Of which: urban registrants (line (1) × 70% [1])	350	420	630
3. Of which: urban registrants who are unemployed (line (2) × 40% [2])	140	168	252
4. Total urban unemployed (line (3) ÷ 40%) (= line (2))	350	420	630

[1] Percentage derived from a survey of employment exchange registrants carried out in 1968 by the Directorate-General of Employment and Training. [2] Percentage of urban employed who do register, derived from National Sample Survey: nineteenth and twenty-first rounds.

Source: Sudhir Bhattacharyya, direct communication.

a correspondingly large increase in unemployment. It is much more likely that it reflected an increase either in expectations of obtaining jobs through the employment exchange or in willingness of the public to use the exchanges; or, again, that it reflected simply a sudden spread of public awareness of the existence and functions of the exchanges.

An interesting attempt to estimate the volume of urban unemployment in West Bengal has been made by Sudhir Bhattacharyya (see table 28) using an approach outlined by J. Krishnamurty.[1] On the basis of the results of a survey of employment exchange registrants carried out in 1968 by the Ministry of Labour's Directorate-General of Employment and Training, Bhattacharyya estimates that 70 per cent of the total number of registrants are urban registrants and that only 40 per cent of these urban registrants are unemployed, the remainder being either students or already employed. Bhattacharyya also estimates, on the basis of the National Sample Survey[2], that about 40 per cent of all urban unemployed do register with the employment exchanges. Since the last two percentages are the same, the estimated number of the urban unemployed would appear to be equal to the estimated number of urban registrants. Bhattacharyya thus estimates the total number of urban unemployed persons in West Bengal at 350,000 in 1969, 420,000 in 1970 and 630,000 in 1971. The sharp rise in 1971 probably implies, however, an increase in the

[1] J. Krishnamurty: "Employment exchange data on unemployment: An attempt at applying correction factors", in Government of India, Planning Commission: *Report of the committee of experts on unemployment estimates* [Dantwalla Committee], op. cit., Appendix III, pp. 145-147.

[2] Nineteenth round (1964/65) and twenty-first round (1966/67).

Table 29. Distribution of job-seekers in metropolitan Calcutta by minimum acceptable salary, according to survey of employment exchange registrants, 1971
(Per cent)

Monthly salary range (Rs)	All job-seekers [1]	Unemployed job-seekers [2]
75-125	1.8	1.6
125-175	12.0	13.7
175-225	22.5	24.1
225-275	25.8	22.9
275-325	25.8	27.7
325-375	5.6	4.8
375-425	5.8	4.8
425 +	0.7	0.4
	100.0	100.0

[1] Average minimum acceptable salary Rs 252 a month. [2] Average minimum acceptable salary Rs 248 a month.

Source: National Council for Applied Economic Research: *Nature of educated unemployment in urban areas* (New Delhi, forthcoming).

proportion of the unemployed who actually register, so that the figure of 630,000 would appear to be an overestimate.

Most of the urban unemployed in West Bengal are to be found in the Calcutta urban agglomeration—perhaps as many as 350,000 at the end of 1971, or 16.7 per cent of the 2.1 million working population of the agglomeration.

A sample survey of registrants at the metropolitan Calcutta employment exchange offices of the National Employment Service, which was carried out in 1971 by the National Council for Applied Economic Research as part of an India-wide study[1], has shown some interesting results. In the Calcutta sample of job-seeking registrants, 31 per cent were already employed full-time, 9 per cent were employed part-time, none were students and 60 per cent were unemployed. In the other large cities of Bombay, Delhi and Madras, the proportion of the unemployed among registrants was 56 per cent, while in the rest of urban India it was 63 per cent. In Calcutta the proportion of job-seekers above the age of 21 was significantly higher, both for all registrants and for those who were wholly unemployed, than in the other three large cities and in other urban areas. The Calcutta sample was unusual in its structure according to educational qualifications. Whereas the dominant group among job-seekers and unemployed in the other large cities and in other urban areas consisted of young persons who had passed their secondary school or matriculation examinations, in Calcutta it consisted of persons who had taken a

---

[1] National Council for Applied Economic Research: *Nature of educated unemployment in urban areas* (New Delhi, forthcoming).

certificate course in engineering; they accounted for 32 per cent of the job-seekers and for 37 per cent of the unemployed among them. The period of unemployment had been much longer in Calcutta than in the other large cities—a difference that seems to point to a higher reservation wage among educated job-seekers in Calcutta than in the other cities. Moreover, the Calcutta registrants were both much more interested in salary and much less interested in social status than those in other large cities. The distribution of Calcutta registrants according to their reservation wage (minimum acceptable salary) is shown in table 29.

TRADITIONAL OCCUPATIONAL CHOICES

It has already been shown that Calcutta's population is composed not only of Bengalis (including migrants from East Pakistan, now Bangladesh), but also of substantial numbers of migrants (or their descendants) from other parts of India, especially Bihar, Uttar Pradesh and Orissa, with the result that linguistic as well as religious origins colour the composition of Calcutta's labour force. Some reference has also been made to the caste affiliations of the Hindu population of Calcutta. It is, indeed, impossible to grasp fully the nature of Calcutta's employment problem without taking into account the influence of geographical origins and caste affiliations on occupational predilections.

For example, in the case of large-scale manufacturing, the jute industry is manned to a large extent by Bihari and Uttar Pradesh Muslims, while the labour force in the engineering industry, including the engineering departments of the jute industry, contains a relatively high concentration of Bengali Hindus. According to data for 1969, jute and paper show the lowest concentrations of Bengalis, while engineering, chemicals, rubber and printing show the highest (see table 30). The proportion of Bengalis among workers in commercial and non-factory establishments was high for the managing agencies,[1] banking and insurance, but (as in shipbuilding) extremely low for inland water transport.

Bengalis traditionally prefer white-collar and skilled jobs. As modern manufacturing developed in Calcutta, they moved into activities requiring greater skills, such as engineering, chemicals and the finer textiles, while the Biharis moved into jute and coarser textiles. At another occupational level, the men pulling the old-fashioned rickshaws in Calcutta are mostly Bihari and Oriya; but, among the bicycle-rickshaw drivers in the suburban areas of metropolitan Calcutta, many are Bengali. Gardeners, plumbers, house servants,

---

[1] See above, p. 25.

Table 30. Geographical origin of workers in West Bengal by sector, 1969
(Per cent)

Sector	West Bengal	Other states					Total
		Sub-total	Bihar	Orissa	Uttar Pradesh	Other	
Factories	*43.2*	*56.8*	*28.1*	*5.8*	*17.1*	*5.8*	*100.0*
Cotton	41.3	58.7	16.5	13.7	21.4	7.1	100.0
Jute	27.2	72.8	37.6	6.8	21.4	7.0	100.0
Engineering	57.9	42.1	20.4	3.7	13.0	5.0	100.0
Iron and steel	40.4	59.6	30.5	1.5	19.8	7.8	100.0
Printing	78.5	21.5	.	.	.	.	100.0
Glass	53.4	46.6	.	.	.	.	100.0
Chemical	67.2	32.8	.	.	.	.	100.0
Paper	30.7	69.3	.	.	.	.	100.0
Rubber	67.3	32.7	.	.	.	.	100.0
Others	47.7	52.3	.	.	.	.	100.0
Commercial and non-factory							
establishments	*58.7*	*41.3*	.	.	.	.	*100.0*
Managing agencies	64.2	35.8	.	.	.	.	100.0
Banking	64.8	35.2	.	.	.	.	100.0
Insurance	69.8	30.2	.	.	.	.	100.0
Import, export, wholesale trade	53.7	46.3	.	.	.	.	100.0
Brokers	60.0	40.0	.	.	.	.	100.0
Traders' associations	100.0	—	.	.	.	.	100.0
Engineers and contractors	58.6	41.4	.	.	.	.	100.0
Manufacturing	54.7	45.3	.	.	.	.	100.0
Airways	46.2	53.8	.	.	.	.	100.0
Shipping	61.6	38.4	.	.	.	.	100.0
Inland water transport	4.0	96.0	.	.	.	.	100.0
Road transport	52.6	47.4	.	.	.	.	100.0
Tramways	52.0	48.0	.	.	.	.	100.0
Power generation	72.1	23.9	.	.	.	.	100.0
Miscellaneous	52.3	47.7	.	.	.	.	100.0

Sources: Government of West Bengal, Labour Directorate: *Labour in West Bengal, 1970* (Calcutta, 1971), pp. 44-48, and Government of West Bengal, Labour Directorate, Statistics Branch: *Handbook of labour statistics, West Bengal, 1970,* op. cit., pp. 9-12.

and *pan* (betel) stall keepers are likely to be from Orissa. Taxi drivers used to be primarily Punjabi but now include some Bengalis and Oriyas. An effort has been made by the Calcutta city authorities to ration taxi licenses to non-Bengalis. As a result, more Bengalis have taken to driving taxis, although some prefer to acquire a licence for its resale value. Tanning and leather working, which are low-caste occupations for Hindus, are largely a Bihari Muslim activity in Calcutta.

Some reference has already been made to the West Bengal State Statistical Bureau's detailed tabulations of persons in various occupations in 1959.[1] In Calcutta city, only 14.6 per cent of leather product artisans were Bengali, while 87.2 per cent of those in printing and related occupations were Bengali. Ship and boat building was largely a non-Bengali activity. Bengalis predominated among the higher levels of clerical workers, but not among messengers and peons. In mechanised manufacturing, skilled workers were predominantly Bengali, whereas among the burden-bearing occupations in the city—rickshaw pullers, handcart pullers, porters—only 5 per cent or less were Bengali.

Several investigators have sought to explain Calcutta's traditional concentrations of specific groups in jute manufacturing and in engineering in terms of caste affiliations and geographic origins. Thus, in a preface to a 1960/61 survey of small engineering units in Howrah, H. Banerji noted that 90 per cent of the owners of the small metal-turning shops were Hindu and that almost half of the Hindu owners were of the *mahisya* caste.[2] A UNESCO report on a 1959/60 study of the small metal-working shops in Howrah also noted that a majority of the owners and workers in the metal-working shops were of the *mahisya* caste, which was described as a caste traditionally associated with agriculture and marginal fishing.[3] The UNESCO report noted, too, that the metal-working occupations did not fit into the existing hierarchy of caste occupations except for the *kamar* (blacksmith) caste, so that *bhadralok*[4] (high status people) could "take up such work, as they could not in the case of weaving and other occupations with a definite caste ranking and low status."[5] The low status of weaving in the Hindu caste hierarchy might also explain the tendency on the part of the Bihari Muslims to move into jobs in the jute mills. In 1946, a report of a labour investigation committee commented on the reluctance of Bengalis, both Hindus and Muslims, to work in any of the unskilled occupations in the jute mills, while as early as in 1931 a report of the Royal Commission on Labour in India had noted that the bulk of the jute mill labour in Calcutta came from the west of Bihar and the east of the United Provinces (now Uttar Pradesh), a tract lying from 300 to 500 miles away from Calcutta.[6]

---

[1] See also below, Annex A, table 42.

[2] Reserve Bank of India: *Survey of small engineering units in Howrah*, op. cit., p. 112.

[3] UNESCO Research Centre on Social and Economic Development in Southern Asia: *Social aspects of small industries in India: Studies in Howrah and Bombay of selected turning shops, blacksmithies and art silk units* (Delhi, 1962), p. 13.

[4] See above, p. 36, n. 3.

[5] UNESCO: *Social aspects of small industries in India*, op. cit., p. 18.

[6] Quoted in ibid., pp. 19, 21.

The occupational concentration of the various groups is reflected in their physical concentration in different parts of the city of Calcutta and of the metropolitan area. A feature of the city that makes this visible even to a visitor is the fact that the slums on the northern and eastern edges of Calcutta are inhabited largely by Bihari and Uttar Pradesh Muslims, who constitute the majority of the factory hands in the jute mills and to some extent in other textile factories. The concentrations of residents within the wards of Calcutta city by language and geographical origin have been mapped and analysed in an illuminating study made by Nirmal Kumar Bose for the Anthropological Survey of India.[1] It would be interesting to see the results of a similar study of the other urban areas of metropolitan Calcutta.[2]

TARGET GROUPS FOR AN EMPLOYMENT POLICY

In many respects Calcutta is, as the title of Asok Mitra's book[3] put it, "India's city". As the industrial, financial and trading centre of all of north-eastern India, it has attracted and employed job-seekers from all over the Eastern Region. Most of the immigrants to metropolitan Calcutta have taken what jobs they could find or have eventually given up and gone home. Consequently, open unemployment has generally been lower among the immigrants than among normal residents. On the other hand, many of the immigrants eventually settle in metropolitan Calcutta with their families and become to all intents and purposes ordinary residents. Furthermore, even though some of the migrants do drift away if they fail to find employment, a substantial number of them still hang on.

Nevertheless, metropolitan Calcutta's central problem is to absorb its long-term residents into productive, or at least remunerative, employment. The primary political concern has to be with the Bengali-speaking residents, since they are clearly a permanent element of the Calcutta labour force (barring an eventual emigration of selected groups if other more rapidly developing areas were to open up). One important unknown factor is the current status of the East Pakistan refugees of the 1950s and 1960s—a question to which an answer will be perhaps given in one or the other of the labour force surveys now being carried out or planned.

---

[1] Nirmal Kumar Bose: *Calcutta, 1964: A social survey* (Bombay, Lalvani, 1968). See particularly the maps at pp. 95-98.

[2] Some elements of such a study for Howrah are to be found in A. B. Chatterjee: *Howrah: A study of social geography* (Calcutta, U. Chatterjee, 1967).

[3] Asok Mitra: *Calcutta, India's city* (Calcutta, New Age, 1963).

Among the Bengalis, the group who are in the most critical situation are those—particularly the young among them—who have some education and are unable to find "suitable" employment. The essence of Calcutta's present employment problem was indeed, stated well over a decade ago as follows: "Nearly 60 per cent of the unemployed persons belonged [in 1956/57] to the educated vocal section of the community. It is unemployment among the educated persons rather than that among the illiterate working classes which constitutes the crux of the problem in this city. . . . It is the volume of unemployment among persons with some school or still higher education that has made the problem so baffling."[1]

In any near future, the target group of employment policy for metropolitan Calcutta need not be the new arrivals, or potential arrivals, of unskilled manpower from the countryside. As in the past, either they will fit into the lower-productivity and the lower-paid employment opportunities that Calcutta has to offer, particularly if the industrial economy expands at a reasonable rate, or they will drift away.

The main target group must be the young people who are already in the Calcutta metropolitan environment in which they have grown up and to whose ways, both good and bad, they are accustomed; whose expectations have been formed in that environment and whose manual and mental skills or lack thereof are the product of urban Calcutta. The new generation of "educated unemployed", who are a special but expanding group among those young people, includes not only the children of the old Bengali middle classes but also the children of the industrial workers settled in metropolitan Calcutta who have acquired at school and in the urban environment many of the middle-class attitudes towards job status and social status.

A secondary target group must be the educated young people in the smaller towns of West Bengal who will drift into Calcutta if employment opportunities are not created for them nearer home.

---

[1] Sen: *The city of Calcutta*, op. cit., pp. 110-111.

ECONOMIC EFFECT OF URBAN INFRASTRUCTURE DEVELOPMENT

4

In 1966 the Calcutta Metropolitan Planning Organisation (CMPO), which had been set up in 1961, published its plan for the development of the Calcutta Metropolitan District.[1] Although designed primarily as a project for general social and economic development and for an expansion of employment opportunities, the plan also provided for investment in the District's physical infrastructure, including especially water supply and drainage, transport, housing and slum clearance, schools and hospitals.[2]

Except for emergency work on the water supply and drainage system and a moderate amount of highway and airport construction, no serious attempt was made to implement the infrastructure projects of the CMPO's development plan during West Bengal's chaotic years of recession in the late 1960s. Under President's rule in 1970, however, the State Government set up the Calcutta Metropolitan Development Authority (CMDA)[3]—a new administrative organisation which undertook a series of crisis programmes to stop Calcutta's physical decline. These crisis programmes, budgeted at around Rs 500 million per year during the last three years of the Fourth Five-Year Plan period (that is, up to 1973/74), include slum clearance, sewerage and drainage works, street and road improvement and housing development—activities which are intended to be consistent with the CMPO plan of development.

In view of these prospects of implementation of, at any rate, some of the CMPO's 1966 schemes for improving the Calcutta Metropolitan District's physical infrastructure, it is proposed to examine in this chapter two implica-

---

[1] See above p. 3, n. 1.

[2] For particulars of these investment plans, see below, Annex B.

[3] The CMDA is a statutory body set up by the West Bengal State Government in September 1970 under a Calcutta Metropolitan Development Authority Act which came into effect in August 1970 under President's rule. With the re-establishment of state government in West Bengal after the elections of March 1972, the CMDA came under the direct authority of the Chief Minister of West Bengal. See also below, Annex B, pp. 122-124.

tions of development of that infrastructure that are relevant to employment in metropolitan Calcutta. One of them relates to the multiplier effects on demand resulting from the initial impact of urban development expenditures. The other relates to the increases in economic activity that are likely to occur as a result of halting the physical and social deterioration of the metropolis, or, to put it in more positive terms, of initiating Calcutta's urban renaissance.

INCOME AND DEMAND EFFECTS OF URBAN INFRASTRUCTURE INVESTMENT

Several questions arise when considering the income and demand effects of urban infrastructure investment; namely first, the relative extent to which the direct income effects are transmitted within metropolitan Calcutta, on the one hand, and immediately siphoned off outside the area, on the other; secondly, the areas to which the newly generated direct demand (urban development expenditures) and indirect demand (consumption and inter-industry demand) will be directed; and thirdly the extent to which the increased demand can be met by increases in real output instead of by a rise in prices. What has to be considered, in other words, is the extent to which the newly generated demand is likely to be met by increases in production within metropolitan Calcutta, the extent to which it is likely to be met by increases in production elsewhere in India and the extent to which it will spill over into demand for imports and into inflationary pressure on prices.

To carry out this kind of analysis properly would require a regional input-output table for the Calcutta Metropolitan District that separated the locally produced inputs to each sector from those brought in from outside. Inter-industry tables constructed for metropolitan Calcutta during the 1960s, including in particular the elegant little "four-sector demonstration input-output table" for 1962 presented by A. N. Bose in his capacity utilisation study[1], do not make this kind of breakdown. Indeed the input-output tables for India as a whole prepared by the perspective planning division of the Planning Commission of the Government of India[2] suffer from the same drawback: imports from the rest of the world appear as a column of negative entries to final demand in the table instead of as a row of inputs. It can be argued that this feature of the all-India table is not an overwhelming defect when analysing the whole of a national economy as diversified as India's. For a region as small as metropolitan Calcutta, however, it is essential to keep

---

[1] A. N. Bose: *Implications of capacity utilisation*, op. cit., p. 41.

[2] Government of India, Planning Commission, Perspective Planning Division: *Draft Fourth Plan: Material and financial balances, 1964-65, 1970-71 and 1975-76* (New Delhi, 1966).

Table 31. Input structure of construction industry, India, 1964

Item	Per cent
Non-industrial materials	8
Iron and steel, non-ferrous metals, metal products	25
Cement	7
Ceramics, bricks, glass	9
Wood products, timber, other forest products	12
Petroleum products, paints and varnishes	2
Total material inputs	63
Value added	37
Value of output of construction industry.	100

Source: Government of India, Planning Commission, Perspective Planning Division: *Draft Fourth Plan: Material and financial balances, 1964-65, 1970-71 and 1975-76* (New Delhi, 1966), end chart.

track of the inter-regional input flows. Use of a table without an import row clearly overstates the internal multiplier effect of an initial increase in final demand. In reality, as A. N. Bose put it to the present writer, "the multiplier effects are most likely to be felt elsewhere".

In the absence of a consistent regional input-output table, it is a piecemeal discussion of the income and demand effects that will have to be presented here. What follows is an attempt to look separately at some of the inter-industry effects of urban development expenditures, on the one hand, and at the effects on consumption of increased incomes, on the other.

Inter-industry demand

Since the bulk of urban development expenditures will be for construction, the most relevant piece of inter-industry information is the input pattern of the construction industry. One estimate of the input structure of the construction industry is presented in the perspective planning division's inter-industry flows table for 1964.[1] The column for construction assigns 37 per cent of the total value of construction output to net value added and 63 per cent to material inputs, including distributors' margins. If the total amount for distributors' margins is allocated pro rata over the material inputs specified, then iron and steel, non-ferrous metals and metal products account for 25 per cent, wood products, timber and other forest products for 12 per cent, ceramics, bricks, glass and non-industrial construction materials for 17 per cent and cement, petroleum products, and paints and varnishes for the remainder (see table 31).

[1] Ibid., end chart.

Table 32. Suggested input factors for selected types of construction
(Per cent)

Input	Highways, sewers, drainage (1)	Highways bridges (2)	Housing High standard (3)	Housing Low standard (4)
Labour	33	30	40	50
Unskilled	22	10	15	20
Skilled	11	20	25	30
Materials	67	70	60	50
Stone, earth, bricks	43	43	37	32
Asphalt	3	3	1	—
Cement	7	8	5	3
Steel	4	6	5	2
Machinery	10	10	5	3
Non-permanent materials	—	—	7	10
Total	100	100	100	100

Sources: Columns (1) and (2): derived from V. G. Bhatia: "Employment potential of roads", in Ronald G. Ridker and Harold Lubell (ed.): *Employment and unemployment problems of the Near East and South Asia* (Delhi, Vikas, 1971), Vol. II, pp. 765-768. Input pattern of sewerage and drainage assumed same as for highways. Columns (3) and (4): rough estimates based on United Nations Industrial Development Organization: *Construction industry*, Monographs on Industrial Development, No. 2 (New York, United Nations, 1969; Sales No. E. 69. II. B. 39, Vol. 2), p. 19.

For road construction, more recent estimates have been made by V. G. Bhatia.[1] Orders of magnitude for some standard factors may be suggested by combining Bhatia's estimates with the general profile of inputs to construction in a "typical" developing country as sketched by D. A. Turin.[2] Bhatia estimates the input composition for the kind of roads that are constructed in urban areas (excluding land acquisition costs) in India at roughly 33 per cent for direct labour costs and 67 per cent for material costs including machinery. For bridges, the labour cost share is lower (30 per cent) and the material costs share higher (70 per cent). Turin's estimates are less specific but would lead to an application of the following standard breakdowns for housing construction: 40 per cent for labour and 60 per cent for material inputs to high standard, or *pucca*[3], housing; and 50 per cent for labour and 50 per cent for material inputs to low standard, or *kutcha*[4], housing (see table 32). For construction

[1] V. G. Bhatia: "Employment potential of roads", in Ronald G. Ridker and Harold Lubell (ed.): *Employment and unemployment problems of the Near East and South Asia* (Delhi, Vikas, 1971), Vol. II, pp. 765-770.

[2] United Nations Industrial Development Organization: *Construction industry*, UNIDO Monographs on Industrial Development, No. 2 (New York, United Nations, 1969; Sales No. E. 69. II. B. 39, Vol. 2), p. 19.

[3] *Pucca* housing is housing built of permanent materials throughout; for example, burnt brick, concrete, stone.

[4] *Kutcha* housing is all housing not *pucca*; for example, with mud plinth and walls, or thatched roofs.

as a whole, the breakdown used by the CMPO in one of its calculations[1] (32-33 per cent for labour and 67-68 per cent for material inputs) seems reasonable.

Of the various material inputs entering directly into construction, probably 70 per cent is produced locally and generates incomes locally; the other 30 per cent represents direct imports into the metropolitan area. Perhaps half of the material inputs to the local production of construction materials are themselves locally produced and the other half imported. Bricks and quarrying products constitute the bulk of construction materials and are locally produced within the Calcutta Metropolitan District, although the wood and coal used for firing the bricks come from outside; there would not appear to be any serious constraints on increasing their production. Cement comes from plants in Bihar and Orissa. Asphalt is imported, and will continue to be so at least until the Haldia refinery is completed;[2] thereafter the import content will be pushed back one stage to crude oil. The steel products used in construction (pipes, concrete reinforcement rods, structural shapes) are likely to be supplied by the Calcutta-Howrah engineering industries, whose raw steel comes either from the Asansol-Durgapur steel mills or from abroad. Unlike bricks and quarrying products, materials such as cement, petroleum products and steel have been in short supply since 1969 when the Indian economy started its recovery from the post-1965 recession. Moreover, they will continue to be in short supply for some years to come unless additional foreign exchange becomes available either from increased exports or from foreign aid. The limitations on supply of these materials will, therefore, impose a first serious constraint on urban construction activity. The extent to which these limitations will affect metropolitan Calcutta will depend, obviously, on the allocations decided upon by the Government of India with regard to the rationing of raw materials.

If the percentages given in the preceding paragraphs are of the correct order of magnitude, the local inter-industry demand multiplier for construction activity is probably close to 1.6; that is, the additional local inter-industry purchases generated by the construction activity will be 0.6 times the initial expenditure on construction, with the effects petering out close to zero by the third round of purchases (see illustrative calculation in table 33). The total labour income generated in construction and in the building materials industries would be in the neighbourhood of 0.6 times the initial expenditure on construction,

---

[1] Calcutta Metropolitan Planning Organisation: *A note on the estimation of employment potential during the Fourth Five-Year Plan period based on CMD development schemes* (1971, typescript), p. 5.

[2] See above, p. 31.

Table 33. Illustrative calculation of local inter-industry demand multiplier for construction

	Round 1: Construction	Round 2: Construction materials	Round 3: Quarrying, etc.	Sum of Rounds 1 to 3
Assumptions:		(Per cent)		
Initial expenditure	100	100	100	
Labour input	33	50	50	
Materials input	67	50	50	
		(Per cent)		
Materials input	100	100	100	
Local content	70	50	.	
Imported content	30	50	.	
Income effect:		(Initial expenditure = 1.00)		
Local expenditure	1.00	0.47	0.12	1.59
Labour input	0.33	0.23	0.06	0.62
Materials input	0.67	0.24	0.06	0.97
Local content	0.47	0.12	0.04	0.63
Imported content	0.20	0.12	0.02	0.34

the direct wage bill accounting for 0.33 and the indirect wage bill for another 0.29 in the illustrative calculation.

The direct employment generation of construction activity may be estimated at about 20 man-years for each Rs 100,000 of construction expenditure (see table 34). The assumptions incorporated into the CMPO estimates cited above yield a figure of about 18 man-years of employment by building contractors per Rs 100,000 of total construction expenditure, in addition to the government administrative staff handling the operation. A less subtle set of assumptions, using the wage rates quoted by V. G. Bhatia[1], yields a figure of 23 man-years of employment for each Rs 100,000 of construction expenditure.

The indirect employment generated locally, corresponding to the indirect inter-industry wage bill calculation shown in table 33, would add 15-17 man-years. The total local employment impact for each Rs 100,000 of construction expenditure would amount, therefore, to at least 33 man-years.

The consumer income represented by the wages and salaries of the newly employed will create further demand for goods and services. The following paragraphs speculate on the direction these additional consumer expenditures will take.

---

[1] Bhatia: "Employment potential of roads", op. cit., p. 766.

Table 34. Estimated direct employment per Rs 100,000 of construction expenditure

A. Cost elements

Item	On CMPO assumptions		On V. G. Bhatia assumptions	
	Rs	%	Rs	%
Total	100 000	100.0	100 000	100.0
Establishment charge	12 500	12.5	.	.
Cost of project	87 500	87.5	100 000	100.0
		100.0		100.0
Cost of material	58 625	67.0	67 000	67.0
Cost of labour	28 875	33.0	33 000	33.0
		100.0		100.0
Profit of contractors	3 609	12.5	.	.
Wages and salaries	25 266	87.5	33 000	100.0
		100.0		100.0
Technicians	1 769	7.0	.	.
Labourers	23 497	93.0	33 000	100.0
		100.0		100.0
Skilled	5 874	25.0	11 000	33.0
Unskilled	17 623	75.0	22 000	67.0

B. Derivation of number of man-years

Item	On CMPO assumptions	On V. G. Bhatia assumptions
1. *Labour cost per Rs 100 000 of construction expenditure* (Rs):		
Technicians	1 769	.
Skilled labourers	5 874	11 000
Unskilled labourers	17 623	22 000
Total	25 266	33 000
2. *Rates of pay* (Rs/year):		
Technicians	3 000 [1]	.
Skilled labourers	1 950 [2]	2 400 [3]
Unskilled labourers	1 200 [4]	1 200 [4]
3. *Man-years* (number) (1. ÷ 2.):		
Technicians	0.6	.
Skilled labourers	3.0	4.6
Unskilled labourers	14.7	18.3
Total	18.3	22.9

[1] Rs 250 per month.   [2] Rs 6.50 per day.   [3] Rs 8 per day.   [4] Rs 4 per day.

Sources: CMPO: *A note on the estimation of employment potential during the Fourth Five-Year Plan period based on CMD development schemes* (Calcutta, 1971, typescript), p. 5; and V. G. Bhatia, "Employment potential of roads", in R. G. Ridker and H. Lubell (ed.): *Employment and unemployment, problems of the Near East and South Asia* (Delhi, Vikas, 1971), Vol. II, p. 766.

Household consumption demand

The pattern of consumption out of additional incomes generated in metropolitan Calcutta will be influenced by two major factors: the general consumption pattern in Calcutta and the specific behaviour as consumers of the groups receiving the additional incomes. Recent information on the general consumption pattern is available from the results of a household consumption survey for Calcutta carried out in 1969/70 by Chitta Mitra and the Research Department of Hindustan Thompson Associates.[1] Speculating about the spending habits of the specific group working on urban infrastructure projects is more hazardous.

The income and expenditure data from the Hindustan Thompson study are presented in some detail in Annex C. The relationships are as expected, with the exception of remittances made, which are surprisingly low. Food consumption in the lowest income categories absorbs as much as 69 per cent of total income, but this proportion declines rapidly as incomes rise, showing an elasticity of 0.7 with respect to income. Within the food group, cereals consumption shows absolute declines at per capita incomes above Rs 100 per month. Non-food consumption shows an elasticity of 1.3 with respect to income; within the non-food group, durable and semi-durable goods show an elasticity of 1.5.

In general, a little over 10 per cent of the increase in incomes accruing to lower income recipients is likely to be spent on food grains. If food-grain production in West Bengal continues to rise as expected in response to the spread of the new agro-economic techniques of the Green Revolution, the supply of this important wage good need not be a constraint on expansion of urban activity in Calcutta.

How applicable the general consumption pattern of Calcutta residents is to the expenditure behaviour of the labour force working on urban infrastructure projects in Calcutta is an open question. In the first place, the construction workers are not usually Calcutta residents. Under the existing system, the contractors who carry out the work normally recruit their construction gangs from rural areas well outside the Calcutta Metropolitan District, usually from the western parts of West Bengal, or from Bihar. The labourers live at the construction site in hutments or tents that they put up themselves, and they keep pretty much to themselves. Since the construction workers normally leave their families at home in the village, the general presumption is that a substantial part of their earnings goes into remittances to the village.

---

[1] Hindustan Thompson Associates Ltd.: *A study of food habits in Calcutta* (Calcutta, Hindustan Thompson Associates Ltd. on behalf of United States Agency for International Development, 1972).

On the other hand, it is also a generally accepted proposition that a considerable proportion of Calcutta's entire working force consists of males living in the metropolis without their families, so that remittances are heavy. There is an oft-quoted comment of Asok Mitra's: "The city annually sends out about Rs 280 million through very small postal remittances: the savings of small men without bank accounts sweating away to keep their families alive in the villages of every state and territory."[1]

The scribe seated outside the post office filling out remittance forms for illiterate labourers at Rs 0.20 per form is part of Calcutta folklore. A. N. Bose has suggested that the remittances made by non-Bengali workers living alone in Calcutta to their families living in rural areas amount to as much as 50 per cent of average income for 44 per cent of the total working force in metropolitan Calcutta.[2] The Labour Bureau's 1958/59 family budget survey of industrial workers carried out by the Indian Statistical Institute[3], showed remittances absorbing about 15 per cent of total income. Of an industrial worker's monthly income of Rs 100 per household (rather than per head) in 1958/59, about 20 per cent went into remittances to dependants.[4]

It would be worth while to carry out a small family budget survey aimed directly at the construction workers in order to find out how they actually do spend their incomes. In the meantime, it seems reasonable to conjecture that they do not differ much in their expenditure pattern from industrial workers at the same income levels in Calcutta. Even itinerant workers must eat where they happen to be, and they are likely to do a good deal of the family purchasing of industrial goods while they are in metropolitan Calcutta. The services they purchase are, however, likely to be rather limited, whereas remittances are likely to be substantial, absorbing as much as 20 per cent of income.

EFFECTS OF REMOVAL OF
SOME PHYSICAL OBSTACLES TO EXPANSION

The major expansion that the infrastructure programme for metropolitan Calcutta is likely to bring about is more indirect than are the inter-industry and consumer demand effects discussed above. It will result from an easing of the physical constrictions blocking Calcutta's economic expansion: choked and inadequate transit facilities, an insufficient water supply, a grossly inadequate number of housing units and deplorable housing conditions. It was this purpose that inspired the preparation of the CMPO's development plan

---

[1] Mitra: *Calcutta, India's city*, op. cit., p. 20.

[2] A. N. Bose: *Implications of capacity utilisation*, op. cit., p. 50.

[3] Government of India, Ministry of Labour and Employment, Labour Bureau: *Report on family living survey among industrial workers, 1958-59, Calcutta* (Simla, 1964), pp. 40, 41.

[4] See below, Annex C, table 59.

during the expansionary years of the Third Five-Year Plan. The report of the 1960 World Bank mission[1] was specifically concerned with the extent to which the failure to solve these problems of the city of Calcutta was putting impediments in the way of economic growth in what was then India's most rapidly expanding industrial region. As the economies of West Bengal and of metropolitan Calcutta gradually recover from the setbacks of the post-1965 recession, the urban infrastructure programmes will become again increasingly important in easing physical constraints on metropolitan Calcutta's economic expansion.

The most obvious bottlenecks have been in transport facilities and in water supply. In transport, the difficulties of moving by road through metropolitan Calcutta are now overwhelming for persons and even worse for goods. The slowness of road traffic undoubtedly raises employment per ton of goods now moved, but it is obvious that both output and employment would benefit greatly from an increase in the productivity of goods movement. The lowering of transport costs should have an expansionary effect on other production. Moreover, ridding Calcutta of its physical transport bottlenecks will not only make possible but will directly induce a rapid expansion of the volume of goods traffic and of employment in transport.

The slowing down of the activities of Calcutta Port owing to the difficulties of moving ships up and down the silting-up channel of the Hooghly is reversible once the major diversion of Ganges water from Farakka is carried out.[2] Improving the functioning of Calcutta Port itself to take advantage of the increase in the flow of water in the Hooghly will also expand goods movement and its indirect benefits. Though the first operation falls largely outside the purview of the Calcutta metropolitan authorities, the second falls within it.

Expanding the supply of water to metropolitan Calcutta along the lines of the master plan for water supply and drainage[3] will not only permit an increase in the availability of water for human consumption; it will also forestall a shortage of water for industrial purposes. The water requirements from municipal piped supply systems for jute textiles, cotton textiles, metallurgy and the myriad other manufacturing activities of metropolitan Calcutta were expected, in the master plan, to grow at almost 3 per cent per year from 1981 to 2001. Without the required expansion of the water supply of metropolitan Calcutta, the continued expansion of industrial activity would eventually be threatened.

Expansion of another important element of the urban infrastructure, namely the housing supply, is also likely to have marked effects on the demand

---

[1] The Michael Hoffman report. See below, Annex B, p. 113.

[2] See below, Annex B, p. 114.

[3] See below, Annex B, pp. 113-116.

for consumer goods, and therefore on their local production. In the first place, increasing the availability of decent housing will cause a shift in the structure of household spending patterns. Moreover, for middle-class urban residents, increased availability of decent dwelling units at "reasonable" prices is likely to bring about the increase in the share of total income spent on housing counted on by Kingsley and Kristof,[1] perhaps by reducing liquid savings, perhaps by reducing other consumer expenditure. Furthermore, the increased availability of housing will create a demand for additional furnishings which will become effective, initially, only if savings or other consumer expenditures are reduced. However, since many of the items of household furniture and furnishing are likely to be locally produced within metropolitan Calcutta, to a considerable degree with indigenous materials, an increase in demand for such furnishings should have a stimulating effect both on local production and on further local generation of income and demand.

Nor should the effects of these physical improvements on morale be overlooked. The despair and despondency which intensified Calcutta's stagnation at its worst can be and indeed are being dissipated by an active urbanisation programme. It may be asserted, although it is obviously not amenable to *a priori* proof, that elimination of the physical bottlenecks choking metropolitan Calcutta will lead not only to directly linked increases in economic activity but also to increases in private investment resulting from a return of confidence in the future of the metropolis.

---

[1] G. Thomas Kingsley and Frank S. Kristof: *A housing policy for metropolitan Calcutta*, A recommendation to the Ford Foundation Advisory Planning Group with the Calcutta Metropolitan Planning Organisation (Calcutta, 1971). See Annex B below for a summary of the report (p. 119).

THE EMPLOYMENT PROBLEM
AND ITS SOLUTION
5

SCOPE OF THE PROBLEM

Some notion of the present dimension of the Calcutta Metropolitan District's employment problem was given in chapter 3, where it was estimated that more than 15 per cent of the District's labour force may have been unemployed at the end of 1971. The future dimension of the problem will depend on the relative rates of growth of local employment opportunities and of the District's labour force. These two aspects of the problem are, however, interconnected inasmuch as the size of metropolitan Calcutta's labour force will vary with changes in local employment conditions.

Metropolitan Calcutta's labour force has grown in response both to increases in total population, in turn affected both by the natural growth of the population already in the area and by net immigration, and to rises in labour force participation rates. Of these factors, net immigration and rates of labour force participation (particularly female participation) are both affected by the level of local unemployment; and, over the 1961-71 decade, they both tended to be held down by the high levels of unemployment. In 1966, the Calcutta Metropolitan Planning Organisation made several projections of population growth for the Calcutta Metropolitan District. The lowest projected rate of growth was 2.4 per cent per year—a rate that included an increase of 0.6 per cent per year due to net immigration.[1] The actual rate of growth of the population of the Calcutta urban agglomeration[2] over the 1961-71 decade, as reported in the 1971 Census, was only 2 per cent per year, or considerably lower than the CMPO's lowest and "most likely" projection. No small part of the shortfall may be reasonably attributed to a slowing down of immigration in response to the worsening employment situation in metro-

---

[1] CMPO: *Basic development plan for the Calcutta Metropolitan District, 1966-1986*, op. cit., p. 69.

[2] See above, p. 35.

politan Calcutta at the end of the 1960s. The 1971 Census also recorded a decline over the decade in the female participation rate for the Calcutta urban agglomeration; but, owing to a 1971 Census change in the 1961 Census definition of the working population, the true decline cannot be distinguished from the apparent decline.[1]

Another aspect of a rate of population growth that is lower in the Calcutta urban agglomeration than elsewhere in West Bengal[2] may be noted in passing. The Calcutta urban agglomeration would be expected to show a rate of natural growth of population lower than the rate in rural West Bengal because of its disproportionately low ratio of females to males. A sizeable percentage of the males working in Calcutta produce their offspring elsewhere, and it may be presumed that the latter stay with their mothers until they reach working age, so that a likely movement of people into town is delayed until they actually enter the labour force.

Presumably, too, future efforts to reduce unemployment levels in metropolitan Calcutta will have an effect reversing the one experienced during the 1960s: immigration to metropolitan Calcutta will be stimulated and female labour force participation rates will be raised. Something like the CMPO's "most likely" population growth projection of 2.4 per cent per year may be expected, therefore, for the 1970s even though it was too high for the 1961-71 decade, while the metropolitan labour force is likely to increase somewhat faster, for example by 2.5 per cent per year.

Employment policy must be geared to some such rate of growth of metropolitan Calcutta's labour force while at the same time aiming at a reduction of over-all unemployment to a more tolerable level. If 5 per cent were taken as a tolerable rate of unemployment, a target for employment creation in metropolitan Calcutta would be given by combining the 2.5 per cent annual rate of growth in the labour force with a reduction of unemployment from 15 per cent to 5 per cent of the labour force in 10 years' time, which would require an annual increase in employment opportunities of 3.7 per cent per year. Reducing unemployment in metropolitan Calcutta by only 5 percentage points, i.e. to 10 per cent instead of to 5 per cent of the labour force, would require an annual increase in employment opportunities of 3.1 per cent.

Some of the required new employment opportunities will be created in the organised and unorganised sectors of manufacturing, transport, commerce and services by the natural expansion of the metropolitan economy. Employment creation to that extent will go hand in hand with the promotion of economic development. The employment effect of normal economic growth

---

[1] See above, p. 43.

[2] See above, pp. 34-35.

is not likely, however, to absorb enough members of the Bengali middle-class residents of metropolitan Calcutta to satisfy their employment aspirations. In view of the heavy concentration of the unemployed among the younger members of the Bengali labour force and particularly the Bengali middle classes, special solutions to their situation must be sought.

Calcutta's employment problem is at least in part the result of a combination of structural imbalances: between the growth of the rural economy and that of the urban economy; between the output of the formal educational system and the job market for educated persons; between the urban jobs available and the aspirations of the existing urban labour force. The relative stagnation of the rural economy of West Bengal, Bihar, Orissa and eastern Uttar Pradesh has long been a major cause of rural migration to urban Calcutta. On the urban side, the Bengalis resident in Calcutta have preferred not to accept low-paid and undesirable urban jobs, for example in the jute mills, thus leaving open low-level jobs which could be filled by migrants from rural areas. At a higher income level, the role of the entrepreneur also seems to be one that educated and non-educated Bengalis have, at least in the past, usually not filled, leaving a vacuum that has pulled in trading groups like the Marwaris from outside.[1] At the middle levels, the Bengalis, whose aspirations have been directed toward white-collar and skilled jobs, have crowded into a labour market which has not been expanding rapidly enough to absorb them.

One inevitable change in the industrial structure of Calcutta's urban economy, which will also effect the structure of the labour market, will be a further relative decline of the jute industry. Jute manufacturing may be expected to stagnate while other branches will continue to expand. The jute industry is traditionally manned by immigrant labour, partly because of the Bengali labour force's aversion to employment in the jute mills. Expanding employment opportunities in newer industrial branches are likely to be more attractive to the resident labour force than in the jute mills, thus reducing one element of the imbalance between the supply of personnel from the resident labour force and the demand for labour. The incidence of unemployment in that event will fall more heavily on the rural labour force, whose members will have less scope for profitable migration.

At the same time and thanks to the freedom of geographical movement that exists within India, any major expansion of employment opportunities in Calcutta will increase its attraction for the surplus members of the rural labour force. Only a reduction in the imbalance between the rural and the urban economies through a marked revival of the rural economy could offset that

---

[1] The Marwaris have "their ancestral homeland . . . in the largely desert region of Rajasthan" (Geoffrey Moorhouse: *Calcutta* (London, Weidenfeld and Nicholson, 1971), p. 170).

attraction. In the case of metropolitan Calcutta, the risk that increases in demand for labour may result in even greater increases in the urban labour supply through accelerated immigration may be avoided if the agricultural modernisation of rural West Bengal is also speeded up.

ELEMENTS OF AN EMPLOYMENT STRATEGY

Any coherent strategy for dealing with metropolitan Calcutta's employment problems must have two aims: discouraging the flow of in-migrants from rural areas and increasing employment opportunities in the metropolis. Measures to achieve the latter aim must include at least the following: a programme for restructuring an industrial base which grew up to meet demands that are now declining; the urban development programme whose theoretical framework and practical details have been set out in the CMPO's plan for the development of metropolitan Calcutta; special programmes for employment of the educated unemployed in metropolitan Calcutta and in the rest of West Bengal; and a programme for systematic development of the informal sector.

Developing rural West Bengal

Today, advantage can be taken of a technological precondition governing the application of several of these measures which, only two or three years ago, did not exist: it is now technically possible to transform and modernise West Bengal's agriculture. The effectiveness of the Green Revolution with regard to food grains—new seed varieties, scientific use of fertiliser, and water control, particularly through ground water irrigation—has already been demonstrated in some parts of West Bengal. It will be only a matter of time—a much shorter time if the present plans of the new State Planning Board of the Government of West Bengal for carrying out a comprehensive area development programme[1] can be put into effect—before the Green Revolution spreads to all of West Bengal lying in the Gangetic plain and to other crops such as pulses, jute and cotton.

A paradox inherent in a programme of urban employment creation is the high degree of probability that substantial increases in employment opportunities in metropolitan Calcutta will attract even greater increases in the labour force. The paradox vanishes, however, if there is also considerable improvement in the rural areas where the flow of migrants originates. In the case of Calcutta and West Bengal, the new agricultural technology based on new seeds, water control and fertilisers offers the possibility of bringing about that improvement.

---

[1] Government of West Bengal, State Planning Board: *Comprehensive area development programme*, op. cit.

Irrigation in West Bengal has been traditionally carried out by gravity flow of the surface water available primarily during the monsoon season. Besides leaving agriculture at the mercy of floods and drought during the monsoon season, this practice has severely limited crop production during the dry season. As a result of the geographical situation of West Bengal in the basin of the Ganges, the State's ground water resources are enormous; but their exploitation has scarcely begun. By 1968-69[1], less than 1,200 pump sets and tube wells had been energised in West Bengal, compared with 59,000 in the Punjab and 402,000 in Tamil Nadu.[2] By June 1972, fewer than 1,800 deep tube wells had been drilled in West Bengal; of these, 1,400 were electrically energised.[3]

In other parts of India such as Punjab and Haryana[4] States, the income-generating prospects of introducing the new agriculture have led to a spontaneous increase in private investment in tube-well irrigation, and there has been little need for the Government to do more than provide credit facilities. In rural West Bengal, however, there are structural rigidities which are likely to prevent such a spontaneous development. They include, on the one hand, a social structure at the village level which encourages inertia on the part of the wealthier members of the village society who could afford to make new investments and which blocks any initiative on the part of the poorer villagers and, on the other hand, a fragmentation of land holdings into numerous and scattered small plots which makes it difficult even for the larger land-owners to irrigate enough of their own land with a single tube well to justify the investment.

A determined effort to organise a massive and accelerated introduction of tube wells into rural West Bengal would therefore seem to be necessary. The West Bengal State Planning Board has recently proposed a well thought out programme along these lines and has already begun to implement it on an experimental basis. The State Planning Board's proposal for a comprehensive area development programme[5] calls for "technological consolidation" of compact blocks of land to provide co-operative facilities, particularly power and irrigation, at minimum possible cost and to make available repair and

---

[1] Government of India, Ministry of Food, Agriculture, Community Development and Co-operation: *Agriculture engineering statistics, 1970* (draft), quoted in United States Agency for International Development: *Economic and social indicators: India* (New Delhi, 1972), p. 40.

[2] Formerly Madras State.

[3] Government of West Bengal, Agriculture Department: *Mid-term appraisal of the Fourth Plan*, quoted in Government of West Bengal, State Planning Board: *West Bengal's approach to the Fifth Five-Year Plan (1974-79)* (Calcutta, 1972), p. 41.

[4] State formed in 1966 from the Hindi-speaking parts of the Indian state of Punjab.

[5] Government of West Bengal, State Planning Board: *Comprehensive area development programme*, op. cit., pp. 25-26.

maintenance services close to the individual peasant. For a shallow tube well, all the contiguous 6-10 acres would be dealt with as one unit with respect to irrigation regardless of the ownership pattern of the particular plots of land covered. Equipment-servicing centres would cover wider areas. The unit area development blocks chosen for administrative purpose would be of about 25 square miles, which, in West Bengal, implies clusters of 25-30 villages with a net cultivated area of 10,000 acres.

If the State Planning Board obtains the necessary political support and financial backing to implement its programme, West Bengal's fundamental economic problem may be on its way to solution. The creation of a prosperous agricultural sector in West Bengal will ease all of the state's other problems and make both direct and indirect contributions to solving the urban employment problem. The direct contributions will lie in providing increased supplies of foodstuffs and agricultural raw materials to metropolitan Calcutta and its industries and in increasing demand for urban-produced industrial products. The indirect contribution will be to provide potential migrants with a viable alternative to moving to the big city.

Reconstructing Calcutta's industrial base

Metropolitan Calcutta suffers from a disadvantage faced by many industrial pioneers: an industry oriented toward demands which are often not the most up-to-date and based on raw materials which are becoming obsolete. On the other hand, it enjoys one of the great advantages acquired by the industrial pioneers: a skilled and adaptable labour force. The problem is to find ways of overcoming the disadvantage and exploiting the advantage.

Metropolitan Calcutta's engineering industry has been one of the victims of shifts in demand. Set up to supply heavy castings, structural shapes, railway equipment and textile machinery, it was badly hit by the reduction in government demands for the output of these industries after 1965 and by the recession in private demand. Meanwhile, the newer metal-working industries producing defence goods, electrical equipment, light machinery and hand tools were being set up elsewhere—in Bombay, Poona[1] and Madras. Metropolitan Calcutta's engineering industry will have to adapt itself to new lines of demand: agricultural equipment as the Green Revolution spreads through West Bengal and consumer goods as incomes rise.

Jute manufacturing and pharmaceuticals are two industries suffering from dependence on obsolescent raw materials. Jute manufactures suffer both from fluctuations in the supply of raw jute and from the relatively high cost of raw jute as compared with the new synthetics which have been encroaching on the

---

[1] About 80 miles from Bombay.

international market for jute manufactures with each downward fluctuation in the supply of raw jute. It is hard to see a solution for jute manufacturing other than appreciable improvements in raw jute yields. Pharmaceuticals production in metropolitan Calcutta has the disadvantage of being based on alcohol, whereas modern pharmaceuticals production is based on petrochemicals. Improving Calcutta's position in the production of pharmaceuticals, therefore, will require access to petrochemical raw materials; but a local production base for the latter at Haldia[1] is still several years off.

In periods of expansion, the rate of growth of employment in manufacturing normally falls far behind that of output. As noted above[2], during the period of expansion from 1951 to 1965, output in manufacturing in West Bengal rose by 6.9 per cent per annum while employment in manufacturing rose by only 2.1 per cent per annum, implying an increase in productivity per man of 4.7 per cent per annum. For all of India over the period 1950 to 1964, value added (in constant prices) per production worker increased by 4.4 per cent per year while employment rose by 5.6 per cent per year.[3] With productivity per man rising at these rates, the rise in industrial employment may be expected to continue to fall far behind future increases in manufacturing output. The importance of manufacturing for total employment is, moreover, not diminished by the fact that direct employment in manufacturing may show only moderate increases; the increases in manufacturing output and in total income originating in manufacturing are the catalysts for much of the tertiary sector activity of the metropolis.

There is no lack of proposed prescriptions for stepping up industrial activity in metropolitan Calcutta, but they may be summed up in Sanjoy Sen's call for "ensuring a steady flow of materials, credit and orders" to industry in West Bengal while "creating conditions for the expansion of existing industries and the setting up of new industries".[4] In the future, as in the past, West Bengal's industry will reflect the state of the whole Indian economy and of the Indian Government's economic and industrial policies.

The policies which will most directly affect Calcutta's industrial expansion are the investment programmes of the Government of India, its import and raw materials allocation policies and its industrial licensing policies. The rate at which the central Government increases total investment outlays under the Five-Year Plans is particularly important since West Bengal still contains

---

[1] See below, Annex B, p. 116.

[2] See above, p. 7.

[3] S. V. Sethuraman: "Prospects for increasing employment in the Indian manufacturing sector", in Ridker and Lubell (ed.): *Employment and unemployment problems of the Near East and South Asia*, op. cit., Vol. II, p. 591.

[4] Sanjoy Sen: Welcome address, Seminar on growth of employment opportunities, Calcutta, Indian Chamber of Commerce, 5 May 1972.

a considerable share of the Indian industries producing investment goods. The central Government's decisions in this regard mainly reflect its assessment of the potential inflationary result of investment activity. Similarly, its import and raw materials allocation policies reflect the Ministry of Finance's assessment of the Indian foreign exchange situation. Where there is room for discrimination in favour of, or against, a particular geographical region is in the regional allocation of total investment, import licences and raw materials in short supply. Whether or not it is true that the central Government has discriminated against West Bengal in the past, it is certainly in its power to discriminate in favour of West Bengal if it is considered politically necessary to do so.

Industrial licensing presents a regional anomaly. The Government of India's ideological commitment to restricting the activities of the larger industrial firms is directed against the concentration of economic power in the hands of the leading private industrial and commercial firms, not against specific regions of the country. As a result, however, of the historical development of modern industry in India, the larger firms, many of them originally British-owned, have been particularly heavily concentrated in Calcutta. Restricting their activities without providing an effective and dynamic alternative has necessarily tended to restrict Calcutta's industrial expansion as well. Calcutta's future industrial growth requires some action in this respect, either by an easing of the administrative procedures relating to the industrial licensing process or by a larger allocation of investment funds to the government-owned industrial enterprises in Calcutta. The former alternative is without a doubt the easier one to implement.

By reason of the pattern of industrial occupations according to language and geographical origin described in chapter 3, the branches of manufacturing best able to absorb elements of the resident Bengali labour force are the older engineering industries and two of the newer branches, electronics and plastics. An increase in all-India investment outlays which raises the demand for the output of metropolitan Calcutta's engineering industries will automatically have a direct positive effect on employment of Bengalis. Encouragement of the newer branches may require more specific measures. For electronics, one of the measures which has been discussed in various quarters is the development of technical training facilities for electronics industry workers. One of the institutions in Calcutta interested in, and capable of, developing such training facilities is the Calcutta Regional Technical Teachers' Training Institute. For plastics manufacturing, a prior requirement is an adequate supply of raw materials. This may call for special provision of imported plastic materials for further manufacture well in advance of building petrochemical facilities for their local production.

The major source of expanding demand for Calcutta's engineering goods lying within the state Government's ability to plan is the expected spread of tube wells and pumps in West Bengal's agriculture. Measures taken to accelerate tube well development and agricultural modernisation in rural West Bengal in the context of the State Planning Board's comprehensive area development programme will quickly have an expansionary impact on employment in metropolitan Calcutta's engineering industries. Although such measures pertain to agricultural rather than urban development, they are of vital interest for industrial Calcutta as well.

Urban infrastructure

As discussed in chapter 4 above, the major direct effects of metropolitan Calcutta's urban infrastructure development programme and any other construction activity on employment are more likely to be felt in rural West Bengal than in metropolitan Calcutta, although their indirect employment effects within the metropolis will be significant. The urban infrastructure programme is nevertheless vital to any employment creation programme for Calcutta since it is also essential to the future economic expansion of the metropolis. Within the infrastructure programme, the sector offering the largest direct and indirect possibilities for employment expansion is housing, but it is precisely for housing construction that funding possibilities are, in the short run, the most inadequate.

The educated unemployed

One special reason for concern with Calcutta's educated unemployed is that the group hardest hit is the Bengali middle class, which comprises an intellectual élite—the *bhadralok*[1]—who have played a prominent role among the factions whose activities have disturbed political life in Calcutta. In so far as economic growth in the Calcutta Metropolitan District will depend on maintenance of a reasonable degree of political stability, some solution of the special problems of Calcutta's middle class will be required.

If the State Planning Board's agricultural development plan is implemented, it will create a large number of jobs for the educated as administrators, extension service workers and entrepreneurs in rural areas. Rural development will absorb educated persons already living in the benefiting areas and may also pull out of town some of the educated unemployed in metropolitan Calcutta.

---

[1] See above, p. 36, footnote 3.

Nevertheless, it will be necessary to have recourse to direct creation of jobs in the organised social services sector. This will involve increasing government expenditure on services such as education and public health. Although job creation by this method may be limited in scope owing to financial constraints on direct government outlays on services and on government subsidies to private social service institutions, it is obviously a socially desirable way of absorbing some of the educated Bengali unemployed. As it is to be hoped that additional financial resources will be made available for these purposes, consideration might be given to the possibility of maximising the number of persons who could be employed under a total outlay on a government social service by reducing non-wage costs, or, more specifically, by reducing investment costs. Consideration might be given also to the possibility of setting up an urban youth service corps with a view to persuading potential employees to accept lower salaries than the norm.[1] It is to be borne in mind in this connection, however, that, as was noted above[2], educated job-seekers have a higher reservation wage in Calcutta than in other cities.

So far as educational services are concerned, the recruitment of teachers is limited not only by the availability of funds to pay them but also by the availability of schools for them to teach in. There are, in fact, two levels of interdependence between school construction and creation of jobs for teachers: on the one hand there is a shortage of physical facilities in which to hold classes and, therefore, to employ teachers, and the other hand the allocation of funds to the construction of physical facilities restricts the availability of funds for recruiting personnel. Although the CMPO's basic development plan calls for a substantial amount of school construction, consideration might be given to a lowering of standards for school premises that would enable more of them to be built with a given amount of investment funds and still provide acceptable facilities. The use of more rudimentary structures and of tents offers a less expensive means of creating teaching space, at least for temporary use, than building standard schools.

The question of the physical standards required to make private schools eligible for government subsidies might also be re-examined. The insufficiency of primary education facilities in the *bustees*[3] is now being partly met in a quasi-spontaneous manner by unaccredited schools run by otherwise unemployed educated young people resident in the *bustees* and financed by small fees paid

---

[1] See ILO: *Matching employment opportunities and expectations: A programme of action for Ceylon* (Geneva, 1971), pp. 197-198.

[2] Page 60.

[3] A *bustee* is a slum area consisting mostly of one-storey low-standard housing. It is defined in the Calcutta Municipal Act, 1951, as "an area of land occupied by . . . any collection of huts standing on a plot of land of not less than 10 *cottahs* [approximately one-sixth of an acre] in area". See also below, Annex B, pp. 117.

by the parents. A modification of the standards for such schools whereby they would become eligible for government subventions would serve both to relieve the precarious existence of these "do-it-yourself" primary education facilities in the *bustees* where no alternative facilities are being provided and to ensure some paid employment activity for the *bustee* school teachers.

There is, of course, an inherent complication in any attempt to alleviate the plight of Calcutta's educated unemployed through an increase in the number of pupils. In the short run, it would seem to be a reasonable measure to absorb some of the existing educated unemployed into the teaching staff of an expanded primary education system in an area such as the Calcutta Metropolitan District, where only 65 per cent of the children of primary-school age are attending school and where, therefore, there is clearly room for considerable expansion of the system. While it may not be possible to prove that the acquisition of literacy enhances the quality of the labour force and can serve, therefore, as a tool for development, it is at any rate clear that, even if it does nothing else, literacy exposes the individual to a wider range of non-traditional influences than he would otherwise experience—influences which should make him better able to cope with, and benefit from, his environment. In the longer run, however, an accelerated expansion of the number of primary-school pupils will expand the demand for secondary-school and university places and eventually cause the supply of educated persons on the labour market to grow even faster than at its present rate of increase.

It was estimated in 1966 that enrolments in the Calcutta Metropolitan District's primary, junior secondary and higher secondary schools accounted for, respectively, 71 per cent of the District's children aged 6 to 10, 55 per cent of those aged 11 to 13 and 30 per cent of those aged 14 to 16.[1] The proportions were, however, considerably lower for children residing in the *bustees*. Increasing the proportions of enrolments by bringing the coverage of free education closer to the official goals of 100 per cent for children of an age to attend the primary and junior secondary schools and 45 per cent for those of an age to attend the higher secondary schools would result, of course, in increases in the proportions of school leavers (including drop-outs) competing for jobs in the urban labour market.

At present the formal educational system turns out persons whose aspirations—and perhaps whose training—do not fit the needs of the labour market. This imbalance can be eliminated or reduced either by changing the aspirations and qualifications of the school leavers or by changing the structure of the labour market as the economy grows. If neither were to change, an increase

---

[1] See CMPO: *Basic development plan for the Calcutta Metropolitan District, 1966-1980,* op. cit., p. 31.

in the proportion of young people passing through the educational system would intensify the future problem of the "educated unemployed".

Changes on both sides of the imbalance are, however, bound to come. With regard to the schools, there is considerable pressure on the part of educators to introduce changes in the curriculum which would give a more practical bent even to primary education. With regard to the economy, the development of new manufacturing industries, the expansion of public and private services and an expansion of the productive elements of the urban informal sector will increase the demand for persons possessing educational qualifications beyond mere literacy, as well as technical skills which can be imparted through the formal educational system.

There is also an obvious social need to expand the medical and para-medical health services, particularly in the *bustees* of Howrah and some of the peripheral localities in metropolitan Calcutta—a need that could be met by personnel already trained or easily trainable if financing were available. Construction of health service premises at lower standards offers the same kind of possibilities for expansion as in the case of schools, though it does raise a more difficult problem of environmental hygiene.

The geographical range of economically oriented social services need not—indeed should not—be limited to metropolitan Calcutta. As the new agricultural technologies spread, there will be a growing need for rural extension services which could absorb large numbers of educated young people. Even if this work did not attract the citified young people out of metropolitan Calcutta, it would slow down the drift of educated young people from the smaller towns of West Bengal to the metropolis by providing creative job opportunities closer to their homes.

Development of the informal sector

It was pointed out above that metropolitan Calcutta's informal sector is both the labour market of last resort for those who cannot obtain "jobs" in the modern sector and an enormous reservoir of productive skills. The goods and services produced by household industries provide a sizeable proportion of the incomes generated in the metropolis. With proper organisation of markets, provision of credit and training facilities and some direct planning, much more of the productive potential of the metropolitan slums could be made a reality.

The re-organisation of agricultural production, as set out in the State Planning Board's scheme for a comprehensive area development programme [1].

---

[1] See above, pp. 29-30.

will make effective an enormous latent demand in rural West Bengal for tube wells, pumps and agricultural implements which can be met by the potential output of the engineering factories and workshops of the Calcutta Metropolitan District. Much of this demand can be met by the smaller workshops of Calcutta and Howrah, particularly if a concerted effort is also made to ensure an adequate supply of raw materials and credit and to organise the initial marketing, through the purchasing network of the Comprehensive Area Development Programme, of agricultural equipment produced in metropolitan Calcutta.

Some initial planning of the production of agricultural equipment in metropolitan Calcutta is called for. As part of such planning, an investigation into the production possibilities of workshops located in the bustees should be undertaken for three purposes—to obtain up-to-date information on existing facilities, to examine the lines of production which can be developed, and to analyse the input, credit and marketing requirements for the organisation of efficient production by small-scale producers.

Such an investigation should cover the production potentialities not only for agricultural equipment but also for other producer and consumer goods. One activity which will inevitably develop by itself, but which can be helped by proper organisation, is a flourishing repair industry.

One of the promising schemes outlined in the CMPO's traffic and transportation plan which should be encouraged is the establishment, once the Kona expressway and the second Howrah bridge at Princep Ghat are completed[1], of a trucking terminal for goods trans-shipment on the periphery of the Calcutta Metropolitan District along the Kona expressway. If constructed on a major scale and if organised efficiently, such a goods terminal could become an important peripheral growth point for the metropolis, drawing some activities and people away from the grossly overcrowded central city and acting as a net to catch some of the new migrants entering the metropolis in search of work. The goods terminal would be a feature of good town planning since it would reduce pressures in the central city; it might also enable new small-scale commercial and handicraft activity in the informal sector to grow more rapidly around it than in the choked central city and could also constitute, therefore, a valuable component of employment policy.

It is the unorganised services in the informal sector which, though the least amenable to policy suggestions, constitute in fact one of the largest users of urban manpower. Laundering, barbering, tailoring, house-cleaning and the other basic services will be provided wherever large groups of people congregate and at whatever income levels the community enjoys. The best guarantee of

---

[1] CMPO: *Traffic and transportation plan for the Calcutta Metropolitan District, 1966-1986* (Calcutta, 1967), A. 152. See also below, Annex B, p. 116.

customers for these services is a multiplicity of household incomes that are too small for the purchase of mechanical household appliances but large enough to command the services of sweepers, laundrymen and tailors. One additional attraction of the metropolis as an employment outlet for unskilled manpower is that it creates a vast demand by both enterprises and individuals for the casual labour and petty services provided by messengers, porters, carters, vehicle pullers and others. It also creates a market for manpower in connection with political rallies, for handicraftsmen at religious festivals and for the practitioners of the more questionable activities in which the big city abounds. As long as a large labour surplus exists, all these unorganised services in the metropolis will continue to absorb large numbers of the unskilled at low rates of compensation. The unorganised service sector will remain one of the manpower markets of last resort.

INTERNATIONAL AID

The international community can help to alleviate metropolitan Calcutta's employment problem by means of the standard aid techniques of financing investment and social programmes and of providing technical assistance in specific fields. One of the obstacles to a general expansion of employment in metropolitan Calcutta is India's more general shortage of economic resources. A substantial international programme to aid the Government of India to implement the CMPO's well formulated development plan for the Calcutta Metropolitan District will lessen this obstacle. Since the greater part of the CMPO's basic development plan and subsequent sectoral plans is formulated in project terms, the traditional project financing approach can be easily followed once the decision to allocate aid resources to Calcutta is taken. The engineering projects clearly embody substantial direct foreign exchange requirements which international aid can cover directly. They also imply local currency expenditures which will be a charge on the national budget. The Government of India will find it politically much easier to allocate these amounts if at least part of the foreign exchange equivalent of the budgetary charge is made available by the international aid donors. There can be no question of India's ability to use the foreign exchange equivalent of such local currency expenditures since they will be exceeded by the indirect foreign exchange requirements for raw materials which the wider industrial expansion accompanying Calcutta's rehabilitation will generate.

In the present state of international relations, the largest parts of the burden of foreign assistance will fall on the World Bank for the improvement of Calcutta's water supply, drainage and sewerage, and on the World Bank and the Soviet Union in the case of transport. There is, nevertheless, considerable room for other bilateral donors in financing parts of the programme. The British have a traditional interest in the bus fleet, whose expansion is in dire need of finance. There are other parts which could be financed by the Federal Republic of Germany, France, the German Democratic Republic and the other prosperous members of the developed world. What may be needed the most is a source of foreign aid financing for housing programmes.

The international community has been involved for over a decade in studies of how to stem Calcutta's deterioration—the World Health Organisation and the United Nations Development Programme through their participation in engineering studies of metropolitan Calcutta's water supply problem, the World Bank and more recently the Soviet Union through their support of studies of transport infrastructure requirements, and the Ford Foundation in its financial and technical support to the Calcutta Metropolitan Planning Organisation in the field of urban planning. It must be strongly urged that the international aid donors should now seize upon the present period of economic recovery and relative political stability in West Bengal as the moment to devote substantial financial resources to supporting the execution of infrastructure programmes.[1]

A pilot programme which could be a model for foreign aid support of social programmes is the proposed UNICEF[2] programme of integrated services for children and youth in the city of Howrah which is being formulated by the CMPO. Under the UNICEF integrated services programme for urban areas (parts of which have also been prepared for Baroda, Bombay and Lucknow it is proposed to combine nutrition, health, education and training activities in selected urban slum project areas on a scale that would enable the programme to make an impact on the neighbourhood. The UNICEF programme has employment implications since it hopes to include and reinforce vocational training activities of the state Government for youths aged 15 to 19 at the neighbourhood level. Eventual replication of the scheme once its practicability has been demonstrated will require substantial funding.

Apart from the technical assistance component of aid to engineering projects in metropolitan Calcutta, the international community has a continuing role to play, both through the International Labour Office and through bilateral aid donors, in providing technical assistance in the fields of vocational and technical training. The newer industries such as plastics and electronics, which give promise of new openings for industrial employment, are prime candidates for such assistance.

[1] On 14 August 1973 the International Development Association, an affiliate of the World Bank, extended a credit of US $35 million to the Government of India to help finance a project in support of the Calcutta Metropolitan District Authority's programme for rehabilitation and improvement of basic urban facilities in Calcutta.

[2] United Nations Children's Fund.

SUMMARY AND CONCLUSIONS 6

Chapter 1. Calcutta, the political capital of India until 1912 and of all Bengal until eastern Bengal became East Pakistan (subsequently Bangladesh), is the only large urban centre in West Bengal, and is also the largest urban centre in India. Its main industrial activities are jute processing and engineering. It also handles as a port a substantial proportion of India's foreign trade. The density of population is exceptionally high, as is the rate of unemployment.

Chapter 2. Calcutta's worst troubles in the late 1960s were closely linked to the general industrial recession which affected all of India in 1966 but was felt most acutely and lasted longest in West Bengal. During the Second Five-Year Plan and the first four years of the Third Five-Year Plan, production and employment in West Bengal's manufacturing industries rose at acceptable rates, particularly in the engineering industries; but the years 1966 to 1969 saw a sharp drop in manufacturing output (particularly again in the engineering industries), with stagnation or decline in employment. Jute processing, which was once West Bengal's leading industry but now is second to engineering, also declined sharply during that period. Instead of absorbing a greater share of an increasing labour supply, the registered manufacturing sector reduced its working force each year from 1965 to 1969; it was not until 1970 that an upturn occurred in total registered factory employment in West Bengal.

Very little information is available on developments in the tertiary sector, which occupies more than half of the working population of metropolitan Calcutta. Information on organised transport, trade and services is sparse, and it is almost non-existent on the unregistered parts of these sectors, which absorb almost one-third of the urban labour force.

Calcutta's economic prospects for the 1970s appear much brighter than they have been for a decade. Political stability in West Bengal, following the overwhelming victory of the Congress Party in the West Bengal state elections in March 1972, is expected to lead to a stepping up of both private and public investment in that state and to encourage a general expansion of Calcutta's economy. In addition, the creation of Bangladesh opens up the prospect of a new set of economic relationships which, at least in the short run, will expand the market for some of Calcutta's products.

Meanwhile, the spread of high-yielding cereals throughout rural West Bengal offers the twofold prospect of easing the problem of the supply of Calcutta's primary wage goods (food grains) and of a vast expansion of rural demand for tube wells and pump sets which Calcutta's engineering industries could produce. The major obstacle in the latter connection would appear to be raw material shortages that continue to limit the growth of India's industrial output.

Chapter 3. The available information on the migration and employment patterns of metropolitan Calcutta indicates that they are intimately linked. However, it is not at all clear whether unemployment is a direct consequence of immigration to the metropolis. The evidence appears to suggest that new migrants take whatever employment they can find and that, when the prospects of finding employment are as bad as they were in the late 1960s, the flow of migrants slows down considerably. The latter point is borne out by the preliminary tabulations of the 1971 Census of India, which show a marked decline after 1961 in the rate of growth of population in the Calcutta urban agglomeration as compared with the rate in the preceding decade. As in that earlier decade, the rate of growth of population after 1961 was considerably lower in the Calcutta urban agglomeration than in rural West Bengal. On the other hand, in the districts including and contiguous to the Calcutta urban agglomeration, the population growth rate was almost as high as in rural West Bengal, so that a further reservoir of potential members of the urban labour force of metropolitan Calcutta may be building up there.

Calcutta receives two kinds of migrant streams: seasonal migrants from rural areas in the off-peak periods of the annual agricultural cycle and more or less permanent migrants who settle in the metropolitan area with or without their families. The permanent migrants include two broad groups: those who have traditionally come in search of jobs or of the other positive attributes of the big city and emigrants from East Pakistan during the quarter of a century or so of its existence. The "traditional" migrants usually come without their families. Consequently, they differ from Calcutta's residents of longer standing in that they comprise a much higher proportion of persons of working age and show a much lower female to male ratio. They are also heavily weighted with non-Bengalis, since the major sources of migration to metropolitan Calcutta are two of the states bordering on West Bengal (Bihar and Orissa) and the eastern part of one of the non-contiguous states (Uttar Pradesh). A considerable proportion of the migrants from Bihar and Uttar Pradesh are Muslim. The emigrants from East Pakistan, on the other hand, are Bengali-speaking and predominantly Hindus of the middle and upper castes; their demographic characteristics are similar to those of the resident population of Calcutta, except that they are a better educated group than the residents.

The industrial and occupational employment patterns in metropolitan Calcutta are closely correlated with the geographical and linguistic origins of the working population. This is most evident in manufacturing: in the jute mills, the workforce is predominantly from Bihar and Uttar Pradesh and largely Muslim, while in the engineering industries it is predominantly Bengali. The lower-skilled urban jobs are most often filled by non-Bengalis, the higher-skilled and professional jobs by Bengalis.

The pattern of employment in terms of geographical origin has its corollary in the pattern of unemployment. Among "traditional" migrants unemployment rates have been much lower than among the resident population, whereas among emigrants from East Pakistan they have been much higher. The migrants arriving from Bihar, Uttar Pradesh and Orissa in search of work evidently took what employment they could find. The emigrants from East Pakistan, on the other hand, arrived mostly in the worst of conditions, in very large numbers at the most critical periods and, to a considerable extent, with middle-class aspirations; their integration into the economic life of metropolitan Calcutta has consequently been long drawn out, painful and incomplete.

A recent estimate of open unemployment based on the number of applicants on the live register of the National Employment Service offices in metropolitan Calcutta puts the over-all rate (unemployed as percentage of the labour force) at something over 15 per cent at the end of 1971. For some groups the rates range much higher. Over the several surveys unemployment rates for the resident population have been higher among the more educated than among the less educated, and higher among the younger age groups than among the older. With rising levels of education and an increasing proportion of young people in metropolitan Calcutta's growing population, unemployment among those groups is becoming increasingly critical.

Chapter 4. The conclusion that emerges from an examination of a development of Calcutta's urban infrastructure, proposed in a plan issued in 1966 by the Calcutta Metropolitan Planning Organisation (CMPO), is that the main effect of urban infrastructure investment on employment in metropolitan Calcutta is likely to be through the expansion of activities now blocked by the physical deterioration of the city. Expansion and decongestion of the transport system and a major expansion of the housing supply have the greatest potential in this respect.

Chapter 5. Any coherent strategy for dealing with Calcutta's employment problems must have two aims, discouraging the flow of immigrants from rural areas and increasing employment opportunities in the metropolis. Measures to achieve the latter aim must include at least the following: a programme for restructuring an industrial base which grew up to meet demands that are now declining; the urban development programme set out in the above-mentioned CMPO plan for metropolitan Calcutta; special programmes for employing the educated unemployed in metropolitan Calcutta and in the rest of West Bengal; and a programme for systematic development of the informal sector.

The technological precondition governing the implementation of several of these measures can be fulfilled, i.e. it is technically possible to transform and modernise West Bengal's agriculture. The effectiveness of the Green Revolution in the production of wheat and rice, through new seed varieties, scientific use of fertiliser, and water control, particularly through ground water irrigation, has already been demonstrated in some parts of West Bengal. It is only a matter of time before the Green Revolution spreads to all of West Bengal lying in the Gangetic Plain and to other crops such as pulses, jute and cotton.

Metropolitan Calcutta's engineering industry will have to be adapted to new lines of demand—agricultural equipment as the Green Revolution spreads through West Bengal and consumer goods as incomes rise. In this respect the skills available in the engineering industry should make adaptation easier. What is needed is some new investment and a dependable supply of steel and other raw materials. Calcutta's industrial expansion would also benefit directly from encouragement of the newer economic branches such as plastics manufacturing and electronics.

Like any big city, Calcutta has an economy with something of a life of its own; but it operates in a much wider context and its essential dynamism is closely linked both with the regional economy of its hinterland—West Bengal and the rest of India's Eastern Region—and with the national economy.

Calcutta's links with the regional economy are two-directional. On the one hand, Calcutta is dependent on wage goods and raw materials produced in its hinterland—foodstuffs to feed the 8 million people in metropolitan Calcutta, raw jute which is processed in the riverside jute textile mills, tea from northern West Bengal and Assam which is packed and exported through Calcutta port, and coal and steel from the coal and iron belt in West Bengal, Bihar and Orissa. On the other hand, expansion of the regional demand for Calcutta's manufactures as well as of the administrative and financial services which Calcutta supplies will depend primarily on the rate of growth of agricultural incomes in the city's hinterland. At the same time, the intensity of the pressure of migration into Calcutta from rural West Bengal and from the neighbouring states is a function of the level of rural economic activity and of rural employment.

Similarly, Calcutta's prosperity or stagnation is also intimately linked with the state of the entire Indian economy. Over-all demand for Calcutta's manufactures, particularly for heavy metal products, depends on the level of demand at the national level; it reflects the size of the investment programmes of the Government of India, which is both a major customer for metropolitan Calcutta's metal industries and a supplier of funds for locally based investment projects; and Calcutta's industry is also dependent on the central Government's allocations of domestic and imported raw materials. At the same time, but probably to a diminishing extent, expanding sectors of the national economy elsewhere provide job opportunities for some educated and skilled Bengalis in localities outside West Bengal.

By reason of its manufacturing base, Calcutta's economic growth is especially sensitive to the general state of the whole Indian economy and to the economic and industrial policies of the central Government. The two most important among these policies are those relating to investment, which directly affect demand for the output of metropolitan Calcutta's engineering industries, and to industrial licensing, various aspects of the administration of which have in the past discriminated against Calcutta.

Calcutta's troubles are in part a reflection of several structural imbalances, between an only slowly growing agricultural economy in its rural hinterland and a normally more dynamic growth of its own urban economy; between the kinds of urban jobs available and the aspirations of the existing urban labour force; and between the output of the formal educational system and the job market for educated persons.

This last imbalance, which results in an undesirable degree of unemployment among Calcutta's educated Bengali middle classes, may be at least temporarily alleviated by the direct creation of jobs in the organised social services, in particular education and health. Since there are recognised financial limitations, two suggestions are worth considering, namely a lowering of physical standards (and therefore of the investment cost) of the premises housing these services, and the creation of some sort of urban youth service corps in which lower salaries than the norm would be acceptable and respectable despite the high reservation wage of Calcutta job-seekers.

Implementation of the West Bengal State Planning Board's agricultural development plan would create a large number of jobs for the educated as administrators, extension service workers and entrepreneurs in rural areas.

Rural development will absorb educated persons already living in the areas affected, and it may pull out of town some of the educated unemployed in metropolitan Calcutta.

Metropolitan Calcutta's informal sector is both the labour market of last resort for those who cannot obtain jobs in the modern sector and an enormous reservoir of productive skills. With proper organisation of markets, provision of credit and training facilities and some direct planning, much more of the productive potential of the metropolitan slums could be made a reality.

The enormous latent demand in rural West Bengal for tube wells, pumps and agricultural implements means that there is a very large potential market for an output of these products from Calcutta's engineering industries. There is a need, therefore, for an inquiry into all possibilities of producing agricultural equipment in the factories and workshops of the Calcutta Metropolitan District.

One main conclusion that emerges from this study of metropolitan Calcutta is that owing to the practice of recruiting construction workers in the countryside the direct employment effects of an urban infrastructure investment programme will be felt by the rural labour force rather than by the urban labour force; the indirect effects on the labour force, deriving from material inputs in the construction industry and from the consumer expenditure of construction workers, will also be limited. However, the indirect effects of such a programme in breaking through the urban bottlenecks hampering expansion of activities are likely to be considerable.

Moreover, with such a programme there is bound to be a significant interaction between urban development and rural development in West Bengal. An expanding agricultural sector in rural West Bengal is essential for an increase both in the supply of wage goods to Calcutta and in the demand for manufactured goods (for example, tube wells and pump sets) which can be produced by Calcutta's engineering industry. On the other hand the expansion of Calcutta's economy will mean continued absorption of former members of the rural labour force, whose remittances to their villages have a significant, even if marginal, effect on rural living standards.

There is clear evidence of an interaction between the state of the labour market in metropolitan Calcutta and the flow of rural migrants into the metropolis. There is thus a strong probability that urban prosperity in Calcutta will lead to an accelerated rate of immigration. However, the opportunity of bringing the Green Revolution to all of rural West Bengal offers, for the first time, a fair prospect of balanced growth in West Bengal's countryside and in the urbanised parts of the Calcutta Metropolitan District.

It has been recognised for some considerable time now that Calcutta's problems can no longer be dealt with at a strictly local level. In 1970 the Government of India initiated the creation of the Calcutta Metropolitan Development Authority and provided it with substantial financial support for improving the urban infrastructure. The major constraint on the resurgence of Calcutta nevertheless remains the limited amount of resources that India can allocate to it. This constraint could be diminished if the international community were to make available additional financial resources and technical assistance for Calcutta through established bilateral and multilateral aid schemes. The international community has been involved for over a decade in studies of ways of halting Calcutta's deterioration; is time for a major transfer of resources that would enable the recommendations made in some of these studies to be applied.

ANNEX A. SAMPLE SURVEYS OF EMPLOYMENT AND UNEMPLOYMENT

Calcutta, Indian Statistical Institute, 1953 [1]

This sample survey, which was carried out by the Indian Statistical Institute in September-December 1953, covered the area under the jurisdiction of the Calcutta Corporation excluding certain special areas such as railway colonies, police and military barracks, hospitals, big hotels and factories. The 1951 Census estimate of the population in that area was 2.46 million, compared with a population of 2.55 million for all of Calcutta city within its 1951 boundaries (that is, without Tollygunge) [2] and a population of 5.4 million within the entire Calcutta Metropolitan District as it was to be defined by the Calcutta Metropolitan Planning Organisation in 1966. [3]

The reference period for the survey was one day (the day of the inquiry). The labour force was defined, with no lower age limit, to include the employed (all those at work for pay or profit, and those with a job but not at work on the day of the inquiry) and the unemployed (those who did not work at all on the day of the inquiry and were looking for work, as well as "persons earning a meagre amount in a casual way but looking for some substantial means of livelihood"). Among persons excluded from the labour force were family members engaged in domestic work, *rentiers* and pensioners, beggars and persons living on charity and remittances, students, and persons either not looking for work or unable to work. Implicitly, pavement dwellers with no fixed residence were excluded from the survey. [4]

A three-stage stratification was used to draw the sample households. The number of households sampled came to about 4,500, drawn as four independent interpenetrating sub-samples.

The distribution of the population by sex and by activity status is shown in table 35, from which it can be calculated that the unemployment rates (unemployment divided by labour force) was 18.0 per cent for all persons, 18.3 per cent for males and 12.1 per cent for females. Distributions of the employed and unemployed population by education level, migrant status and age group are shown in tables 36 to 38.

Calcutta, Calcutta University, 1954/58 [5]

This sample survey, which was carried out by Calcutta University, used a two-stage stratification to draw the sample. The number of households sampled in each annual round came to between 4,000 and 5,000. The economic status definitions were shifted mid-way

---

[1] See above, pp. 46-47.

[2] Incorporated into the Calcutta municipal area in 1953.

[3] See above, p. 3, n. 1.

[4] See *National Sample Survey*, No. 8: *Report on preliminary survey of urban unemployment: September 1953* (New Delhi, Ministry of Finance, Department of Economic Affairs, 1956), pp. 3, 4. These definitions differ somewhat from those used in a preliminary survey of unemployment in urban India, excluding Calcutta, Bombay, Madras and Delhi.

[5] See above, pp. 37-39, 47.

101

Table 35. Distribution of population by sex and activity status, Calcutta, 1953

Industrial status	Male	Female	All
Persons in labour force	*62.8*	*5.8*	*39.5*
Gainfully occupied	51.3	5.1	32.4
Unemployed	11.5	0.7	7.1
Persons not in labour force	*37.2*	*94.2*	*60.5*
Family members engaged in domestic work only	0.8	54.6	22.8
Rentiers, pensioners, beggars	1.4	1.0	1.2
Children, students, old and infirm persons	35.0	38.6	36.5
Total population [1]	*100.0*	*100.0*	*100.0*

[1] Numbers in 1951, assuming sample results applied to 1951 population total: 1,457,500 males; 1,008,600 females; 2,466,100 for both sexes.

Source: *National Sample Survey*, No. 17: *Report on sample survey of employment in Calcutta, 1953*, op. cit., p. 23.

Table 36. Distribution of the labour force by education level and activity status, Calcutta, 1953

Education level	Gainfully occupied	Unemployed	Labour force
A. *Per cent by activity status:*			
Illiterate	25.0	9.9	22.3
Literate, below Matriculation	53.4	63.4	55.2
Matriculation	11.1	18.3	12.4
Intermediate	4.6	5.6	4.8
Graduate	5.9	2.8	5.3
Total	100.0 [1]	100.0 [2]	100.0 [3]
B. *Per cent by education level:*			
Illiterate	92.2	7.8	100.0
Literate, below Matriculation	79.5	20.6	100.0
Matriculation	73.4	26.6	100.0
Intermediate	79.0	21.0	100.0
Graduate	90.5	9.5	100.0
Total	82.0	18.0	100.0

[1] Estimated number in 1951, assuming sample results applied to 1951 population total, 799,000.   [2] 175,100, on the same assumptions.   [3] 974,100, on the same assumptions.

Source: *National Sample Survey*, No. 17: *Report on sample survey of employment in Calcutta, 1953*, op. cit., pp. 27, 28, 97.

through the survey. In the first two rounds, a three-way classification was used: earners, dependants, and working dependants. In the last two rounds, a fourth category was split off from earners: non-member employees of a household. An unemployed person was defined as one over 14 years of age with no gainful occupation on the date of the investigation but actively seeking work at current rates of remuneration.

The survey covered a sample population which showed a sex ratio of 533 females per 1,000 males in 1957/58, as compared with the higher sex ratio of 692 to 1,000 in the Indian Statistical Institute's sample survey of 1953 described above.

Table 37. Distribution of labour force by migrant status and activity status, Calcutta, 1953

Category	Per cent by migrant status			Per cent by employment status			Estimated no. in labour force in 1951 [1] ('000)
	Gain-fully occupied	Unem-ployed	Labour force	Gain-fully occupied	Unem-ployed	Labour force	
Non-migrants	*31.9*	*37.1*	*32.8*	*79.6*	*20.4*	*100.0*	*319.4*
Local persons	31.8	37.0	32.7	79.6	20.4	100.0	318.6
Temporary visitors	0.1	0.1	0.1	70.8	29.2	100.0	0.8
Migrants from—	*68.1*	*62.9*	*67.2*	*83.2*	*16.8*	*100.0*	*654.7*
Rural W. Bengal	11.2	8.1	10.6	86.4	13.6	100.0	103.4
Urban W. Bengal	3.1	2.3	3.0	86.0	14.0	100.0	29.2
Rural areas in other states	25.4	9.7	22.5	92.2	7.8	100.0	219.6
Urban areas in other states	4.9	3.5	4.7	86.6	13.4	100.0	45.4
East Pakistan as displaced persons	13.1	34.4	17.0	63.4	36.6	100.0	165.5
East Pakistan before Partition	8.7	4.7	8.0	89.3	10.7	100.0	77.6
Other places	1.7	0.2	1.4	97.3	2.7	100.0	14.0
Total	*100.0*	*100.0*	*100.0*	*82.0*	*18.0*	*100.0*	*974.1*

[1] Assuming sample results apply to 1951 total population.

Source: *National Sample Survey*, No. 17: *Report on sample survey of employment in Calcutta, 1953*, op. cit., pp. 30, 31.

Table 38. Activity status of the labour force by age group, Calcutta, 1953
(Per cent of labour force)

Age group	Gainfully occupied	Unemployed			Labour force
		1st time	Not 1st time	All	
7-15	71	29	.	29	100
16-21	60	35	5	40	100
22-26	72	17	11	28	100
27-36	89	2	9	11	100
37-46	91	1	8	9	100
47-56	91	2	7	9	100
57-61	89	.	11	11	100
62 +	83	.	17	17	100
7 +	82	10	8	18	100

Source: *National Sample Survey*, No. 17: *Report on sample survey of employment in Calcutta, 1953*, op. cit., pp. 26, 66.

As shown in table 39, the over-all unemployment rate (unemployment as percentage of the labour force) recorded in the survey declined from 10.0 per cent in 1954/55 to 7.6 per cent in 1956/57, a movement that probably reflected the quickening trend of economic activity about the time of the start of India's Second Five-Year Plan. The rates calculated in the survey report by age group, by migrant status and by level of educational attainment are also shown in the same table.

Table 39. Unemployment rates by age group, migrant status and education level, Calcutta, 1954/55-1956/57
(Unemployment as per cent of labour force [1])

Category	1954/55	1955/56	1956/57
Total (age 15 and over)	10.0	9.2	7.6
By age group:			
15-19	41.6	36.0	30.0
20-24	21.2	21.4	15.3
25-29	7.2	6.3	5.5
30-34	3.4	4.1	3.2
35-44	4.8	2.3	3.0
45-59	2.3	2.7	4.7
By migrant status:			
Original residents	.	10.0	8.5
All migrants	.	8.2	6.2
Ordinary migrants	.	5.3	5.0
Displaced migrants	.	20.2	12.2
By educational level:			
Illiterates	3.5	3.4	4.3
Literates	6.0	5.2	5.1
Upper primary, lower primary	7.7	11.5	8.1
School education below school final . . .	17.0	18.7	12.7
School final and undergraduates	16.5	14.0	9.8
Graduates	5.0	8.5	5.2
Postgraduates	8.8	3.3	2.3

[1] Sen uses the item "job-seeking population" rather than "labour force".

Source: Sen: *The city of Calcutta,* op. cit., pp. 109, 111, 112.

Calcutta and surrounding industrial areas, West Bengal State Statistical Bureau, 1959 [1]

This sample survey of unemployment, which was carried out by the West Bengal State Statistical Bureau in April-July 1959, covered the industrial areas surrounding Calcutta as well as Calcutta city. The industrial areas included Asansol, which is located 120 miles beyond the boundaries of the region referred to in the present study as the Calcutta Metropolitan District. The total population at the time of the survey was estimated at 2.97 million persons in Calcutta (including Tollygunge) and at 5.45 million in Calcutta and the industrial areas (including Asansol) combined. The sample, which was a large one (2 per cent in Calcutta and 2.5 per cent in Tollygunge and the industrial areas including Asansol), was arrived at by a two-stage sampling procedure. The total number of families listed in the first stage of the inquiry came to close to 300,000. The total number of families surveyed at the second stage was over 30,000: 14,000 in Calcutta and over 16,000 in Tollygunge and the industrial areas including Asansol. The reference period used was the week (7 days) prior to the inquiry. The labour force was defined to include (*a*) all those with full-time employment during any one or more days of the reference week and (*b*) persons with no

[1] See above, pp. 47-48.

Table 40. Distribution of population by sex and activity status, Calcutta and surrounding industrial areas, 1959

Item	All ages			Age groups 16-60		
	Male	Female	Total	Male	Female	Total
A. Calcutta (incl. Tollygunge):						
Millions:						
Population	1.84	1.13	2.97	1.34	0.68	2.02
Labour force (LF)	1.26	0.10	1.36	1.22	0.10	1.32
Unemployment	0.13	0.03	0.16	0.13	0.03	0.16
Per cent:						
LF: Population	68.5	8.8	45.8	91.0	14.7	65.3
Unemployment: LF	10.3	30.0	11.8	10.7	30.0	12.1
B. Calcutta and industrial areas (incl. Asansol):						
Millions:						
Population	3.35	2.10	5.45	2.39	1.24	3.63
Labour force (LF)	2.24	0.17	2.41	2.20	0.16	2.36
Unemployment	0.25	0.04	0.29	0.24	0.04	0.28
Per cent:						
LF: Population	66.9	8.1	44.2	92.1	12.9	65.0
Unemployment: LF	11.2	23.5	12.0	10.9	25.0	11.9

Source: Government of West Bengal, State Statistical Bureau: *Report on the survey of unemployment in Calcutta and Calcutta industrial areas, 1959*, op. cit., pp. 27, 40, 44, 89, 102, 106.

Table 41. Unemployment rates by sex, education level, and age group, Calcutta and surrounding industrial areas, 1959
(Unemployment as per cent of labour force)

Category	Calcutta, incl. Tollygunge			Calcutta and Calcutta industrial areas, incl. Asansol		
	Non-manual	Manual	Total	Non-manual	Manual	Total
Sex:						
Male	16.1	6.7	10.3	17.2	8.1	10.9
Female	37.8	16.6	27.9	38.7	18.4	27.0
Both sexes	18.3	7.3	11.7	19.2	8.7	12.1
Education level:						
Illiterate	1.7	3.7	3.5	2.7	6.1	5.9
Literate [1]	21.0	9.6	13.4	23.3	10.0	13.4
Educated [2]	18.7	34.2	19.5	18.3	26.3	19.0
All levels	18.3	7.3	11.7	19.2	8.7	12.1
Selected age groups:						
16-20	58.8	25.3	39.1	62.4	30.1	40.9
21-25	36.3	12.2	22.0	37.7	14.9	22.6
26-30	14.3	4.5	8.1	13.8	5.3	7.9

[1] But below Matriculation standard.   [2] To Matriculation standard and above.

Source: Government of West Bengal, State Statistical Bureau: *Report on the survey of unemployment ..., 1959*, op. cit., pp. 12, 13, 14, 48, 110. Percentages are those presented in the original source.

Table 42. Distribution by occupation of Bengali and other earners in Calcutta[1], 1959

Occupation	Earners ('000)			Bengalis as % of all earners	All earners (%)
	All	Bengali	Other		
Professional, technical and related	105.7	84.6	21.1	80.0	8.72
Accounting, auditing	3.9	2.7	1.2	68.7	0.32
Arts, artists	8.6	7.1	1.5	82.8	0.71
Literary	2.1	1.8	0.3	86.2	0.17
Teaching, training	26.5	21.5	5.0	81.1	2.19
Legal	3.8	3.5	0.3	91.2	0.31
Engineer, technologist	8.5	6.5	2.0	76.8	0.70
Technical assistant	29.1	23.4	5.7	80.5	2.40
Research, experiments	0.4	0.3	0.1	83.1	0.03
Medical, health services	14.7	12.9	1.8	87.2	1.21
Miscellaneous	8.1	4.9	3.2	60.5	0.67
Owners, tenants, managers, officials (agriculture and related), non-technical n.e.c. [2]	2.6	1.8	0.8	69.5	0.21
Agriculture, horticulture	0.6	0.5	0.1	88.9	0.05
Plantation	0.8	0.4	0.4	49.9	0.07
Animal husbandry, forestry, fishing	0.9	0.6	0.3	66.7	0.07
Mines	0.3	0.3	—	100.0	0.02
Owners, managers, officials (excluding agriculture and related), non-technical	57.7	35.8	21.9	62.0	4.76
Clerical and related	197.4	148.8	48.6	75.4	16.28
Accounts	20.6	13.5	7.1	66.0	1.70
General	129.1	110.5	18.6	85.5	10.65
Messenger, carrier	30.6	12.3	18.3	40.2	2.52
Operator	3.2	2.4	0.8	76.0	0.26
Other n.e.c. [2]	13.9	10.1	3.8	72.5	1.15
Sales workers	210.7	106.5	104.2	50.5	17.38
Sales	188.6	96.2	92.4	51.0	15.56
Sales services	18.8	8.2	10.5	44.1	1.55
Others	3.3	2.0	1.3	61.1	0.27
Handicraftsmen (mainly manual)	160.0	97.1	62.9	60.5	13.20
Food, beverage, tobacco, etc.	28.0	15.8	12.2	56.4	2.31
Textiles	6.0	3.0	3.0	49.2	0.49
Garments and related textile products	25.1	16.5	8.6	65.8	2.07
Leather products	21.7	3.2	18.5	14.6	1.79
Wood, cane and bamboo work and related occupations	24.3	17.3	7.0	71.2	2.01
Printing, binding and related occupations	13.4	11.6	1.8	87.2	1.11
Metal and general engineering and related occupations	24.5	17.9	6.6	73.0	2.02
Ship building, boat building	0.4	0.1	0.3	13.7	0.03
Miscellaneous	16.6	11.7	4.9	68.7	1.37

(table continued opposite)

Occupation	Earners ('000)			Bengalis as % of all earners	All earners (%)
	All	Bengali	Other		
Operatives (mainly mechanised)	29.3	10.7	18.6	36.6	2.42
Transport operation	23.0	7.6	15.4	33.0	1.90
Metal and general engineering and related	4.2	1.9	2.3	45.4	0.35
Electrical and related	2.1	1.2	0.9	58.2	0.17
Services	213.9	85.1	128.8	39.8	17.64
Essential public service	15.2	8.5	6.7	55.8	1.25
Domestic, personal and related service	152.8	59.8	93.0	39.1	12.60
Other	45.9	16.8	29.1	36.5	3.79
Labour	231.5	73.4	158.1	31.7	19.09
Agriculture and related	6.7	1.4	5.3	20.4	0.55
Mining	0.3	0.1	0.2	66.2	0.02
Skilled labour	0.2	0.1	0.1	50.0	0.01
Unskilled labour	0.1	—	0.1	—	0.01
Manufacturing (mainly mechanised)	36.5	20.5	16.0	56.2	3.01
Skilled	25.8	16.5	9.3	63.9	2.13
Unskilled	10.7	4.0	6.7	37.6	0.88
Manufacturing (mainly manual) except handicraftsmen	48.0	19.9	28.1	41.6	3.96
Skilled labour	29.4	13.6	15.8	46.3	2.43
Unskilled labour	18.6	6.3	12.3	34.0	1.53
Others, specified	35.9	1.6	34.3	4.5	2.96
Cycle rickshaw puller	0.4	0.1	0.3	28.4	0.03
Rickshaw puller	16.3	0.6	15.7	3.8	1.34
Handcart puller	7.0	0.2	6.8	2.5	0.58
Porter	10.9	0.6	10.3	5.6	0.90
Others	1.3	0.1	1.2	5.3	0.11
Others, unspecified	104.1	29.9	74.2	28.7	8.59
Skilled labour	34.3	16.0	18.3	46.4	2.83
Unskilled labour	69.8	13.9	55.9	19.8	5.76
Occupation not reported	3.6	3.2	0.4	81.1	0.30
Total (all occupations)	**1 212.4**	**647.0**	**565.4**	**53.3**	**100.00**

[1] Including Tollygunge. [2] Not elsewhere covered.

Source: Government of West Bengal, State Statistical Bureau: *Report on the survey of unemployment in Calcutta and Calcutta industrial areas, 1959*, op. cit., Table C-23, pp. 126-136.

Table 43. Distribution by occupation of Bengali and other earners in Calcutta and the

Occupation	Earners ('000)			Bengalis as % of all earners	All earners (%)
	All	Bengali	Other		
Professional, technical and related	157.1	127.3	29.8	81.0	7.34
Accounting, auditing	4.5	3.2	1.3	71.2	0.21
Arts, artists	11.3	9.4	1.9	83.6	0.53
Literary	2.6	2.1	0.5	82.9	0.12
Teaching, training	41.6	34.8	6.8	83.7	1.94
Legal	5.1	4.8	0.3	93.9	0.24
Engineer, technologist	11.6	9.3	2.3	80.4	0.54
Technical assistant	48.0	38.0	9.4	80.4	2.24
Research, experiments	0.5	0.4	0.1	86.2	0.02
Medical, health services	19.6	16.9	2.7	85.8	0.92
Miscellaneous	12.3	7.7	4.6	62.1	0.58
Owners, tenants, managers, officials (agriculture and related), non-technical n.e.c. [1]	5.0	4.0	1.0	79.9	0.23
Agriculture, horticulture	2.6	2.4	0.2	93.7	0.12
Plantation	0.9	0.6	0.3	59.6	0.04
Animal husbandry, forestry, fishing	1.2	0.8	0.4	65.5	0.06
Mines	0.3	0.2	0.1	83.5	0.01
Owners, managers, officials (excluding agriculture and related), non-technical	73.9	47.5	26.4	64.2	3.45
Clerical and related	287.8	226.6	61.2	78.4	13.44
Accounts	29.4	21.2	8.2	71.9	1.37
General	190.3	166.5	23.8	87.5	8.89
Messenger, carrier	41.8	18.6	23.2	44.5	1.95
Operator	4.5	3.5	1.0	77.3	0.21
Other n.e.c. [1]	21.8	16.8	5.0	77.2	1.02
Sales worker	313.7	159.0	154.7	50.7	14.65
Sales	287.7	145.7	142.0	50.7	13.44
Sales services	21.6	10.7	10.9	49.5	1.01
Others	4.4	2.6	1.8	59.2	0.21
Handicraftsmen (mainly manual)	271.2	153.2	118.0	56.1	12.67
Food, beverage, tobacco, etc.	41.8	25.2	16.6	60.3	1.95
Textiles	43.2	9.4	33.8	21.8	2.02
Garments and related textile products	48.3	34.2	14.1	70.7	2.26
Leather products	24.7	3.5	21.2	14.2	1.15
Wood, cane and bamboo work and related occupations	35.6	25.4	10.2	71.3	1.66
Printing, binding and related occupations	15.2	13.3	1.9	87.7	0.71
Metal and general engineering and related occupations	36.5	24.9	11.6	68.2	1.71
Ship building, boat building	0.7	0.4	0.3	56.6	0.03
Miscellaneous	25.2	16.9	8.3	65.8	1.18

(table continued opposite)

surrounding industrial areas (including Asansol), 1959

Occupation	Earners ('000)			Bengalis as % of all earners	All earners (%)
	All	Bengali	Other		
Operatives (mainly mechanised)	44.6	17.2	27.4	38.7	2.09
Transport operation	30.6	10.3	20.3	33.7	1.43
Metal and general engineering and related	10.8	4.7	6.1	43.7	0.51
Electrical and related	3.2	2.2	1.0	68.8	0.15
Services	294.2	116.4	177.8	39.6	13.74
Essential public service	28.6	17.1	11.5	60.0	1.33
Domestic, personal and related service	207.2	77.2	130.0	37.2	9.68
Other	58.4	22.1	36.3	31.8	2.73
Labour	688.7	187.4	501.3	27.2	32.17
Agriculture and related	18.2	8.3	9.9	45.8	0.85
Mining	0.6	0.4	0.2	60.9	0.03
Skilled labour	0.3	0.2	0.1	73.2	0.015
Unskilled labour	0.3	0.2	0.1	46.8	0.015
Manufacturing (mainly mechanised)	355.2	77.6	277.6	21.8	16.59
Skilled labour	252.7	59.5	193.2	23.5	11.80
Unskilled labour	102.5	18.1	84.4	17.7	4.79
Manufacturing (mainly manual) except handicraftsmen	73.7	28.5	45.2	38.6	3.44
Skilled labour	41.8	19.1	22.7	45.6	1.95
Unskilled labour	31.9	9.4	22.5	29.5	1.49
Others, specified	54.9	4.4	50.5	8.0	2.57
Cycle rickshaw puller	5.1	1.8	3.3	35.1	0.24
Rickshaw puller	18.9	1.1	17.7	5.8	0.89
Handcart puller	8.4	0.3	8.1	3.3	0.39
Porter	19.7	1.1	18.7	5.4	0.92
Others	2.8	0.2	2.6	6.2	0.13
Others, unspecified	186.1	68.2	117.9	36.6	8.69
Skilled labour	57.4	27.7	29.7	48.3	2.68
Unskilled labour	128.7	40.5	88.2	68.6	6.01
Occupation not reported	4.7	4.1	0.6	87.2	0.22
Total (all occupations)	2 140.9	1 042.7	1 098.2	48.7	100.00

[1] Not elsewhere covered.

Source: Government of West Bengal, State Statistical Bureau: *Report on the survey of unemployment in Calcutta and Calcutta industrial areas, 1959*, op. cit., Table W-23, pp. 64-73.

full-time employment during any day of the reference week and actively looking for such employment. Employment was defined as full-time employment if it averaged more than five hours per day or if it was considered to be full-time. Persons with part-time employment only (i.e. those working less than full time on a single day of the reference week) were considered as unemployed in the tabulating of unemployment rates. Since the sampling unit was the household, persons without a fixed residence (pavement dwellers) were not covered by the inquiry.

Separate tabulations were made for Calcutta City including Tollygunge and for Calcutta and its industrial area (Calcutta, the surrounding industrial areas and Asansol).

The labour force participation rates and unemployed rates by sex, age group and education level, as revealed by the survey, are shown in tables 40 and 41.

The report on the survey contains an instructive breakdown of employed persons by detailed occupational category (see tables 42 and 43), which provide some evidence for allocating the employed labour force to the modern and the informal sectors. The breakdown of the employed into Bengalis and others throws a good deal of light on the occupational structure of Calcutta's labour force according to geographic and language origin.

All India, National Sample Survey, 1955-67

The results of a number of all-India sample surveys of urban employment and unemployment carried out during the 1950s and 1960s[1] showed that the unemployment rates (unemployment as percentage of labour force) in all of urban India were much lower than the rates shown in the above Calcutta sample surveys.

As shown in table 44[2], there was a marked decline in urban unemployment rates for all India from 1957/58 to 1966/67. The decline was, however, partly due to an intervening change in definition from "available for work" to "seeking work".[3]

During the 1950s a separate set of estimates was published in the *National Sample Survey* for each of three urban strata, the first of which consisted of the four big cities (Bombay, Calcutta, Delhi and Madras). The unemployment rates estimated for this stratum were lower than those shown in the Calcutta surveys but were still quite high (see table 45). This stratum was, however, dropped from July 1960-June 1961 onward, when the only separate estimates made were for each state. The figures for all of urban West Bengal (see table 45) were in several cases lower than the all-India urban estimates and also showed a markedly declining trend up to 1966/67, the most recent year in respect of which sample survey labour force data have been published.[4] It may be assumed that the declining trend in unemployment was also felt in Calcutta, though at levels that cannot be determined from the data as tabulated.

---

[1] *National Sample Survey*, Reports Nos. 62 (9th Round), 34 (10th Round), 52 (11th and 12th Rounds), 63 (13th Round), 85 (14th Round), 157 (15th Round), 103 (16th Round), 127 (17th Round), 152 (18th Round), 163 (19th Round), 166 (20th Round) and 181 (21st Round). At the time of completion of the present study, a 27th Round was planned for the period October 1972-September 1973.

[2] The *National Sample Survey* data quoted in table 44 are taken from Pravin Visaria: "Employment and unemployment in India: A review of selected statistics", in: Government of India, Planning Commission: *Report of the committee of experts on unemployment statistics*, op. cit., Appendix II, p. 53.

[3] *National Sample Survey*, No. 152: *18th Round, February 1963-January 1964, Tables with notes on urban labour force* (Delhi, Cabinet Secretariat, 1969), p. 3.

[4] *National Sample Survey*, No. 181: *21st Round, July 1966-June 1967, Tables with notes on urban labour force* (Delhi, Cabinet Secretariat, 1971).

Table 44. Activity status of urban population according to various rounds of the National Sample Survey: All India, 1955-67

NSS round	Period covered	Reference period	As per cent of total population			Unemployed as per cent of labour force
			Gainfully employed (1)	Unemployed (2)	Labour force (1) + (2) (3)	(2) ÷ (3) (4)
9th	May 1955-Nov. 1955	Year [1]	32.44	1.82	34.26	5.31
10th	Dec. 1955-May 1956	Day	32.68	1.98	34.66	5.71
11th	Aug. 1956-Aug. 1957	Day [2]	30.94	2.43	33.37	7.28
12th		Week [2]	31.33	1.83	33.16	5.52
13th	Sep. 1957-May 1958	Day	31.38	2.49	33.87	7.35
		Week	32.18	1.91	34.09	5.60
14th	July 1958-June 1959	Week	31.77	1.18	32.95	3.58
15th	July 1959-June 1960	Week	31.60	1.76	33.36	5.28
16th	July 1960-June 1961	Week	33.19	0.82	34.01	2.41
17th	Sep. 1961-July 1962	Week	31.16	0.98	32.14	3.05
18th	Feb. 1963-Jan. 1964	Week	31.05	0.63	31.68	1.99
19th	July 1964-June 1965	Week	30.96	0.61	31.57	1.93
		Week [3]	32.40	1.18	33.58	3.51
20th	July 1965-June 1966	Week	30.40	0.61	31.01	1.97
21st	July 1966-June 1967	Week	31.42	0.51	31.93	1.60

[1] Usual status. [2] Households other than those classified as agricultural labour households. [3] Data based on the Integrated Household Schedule.

Source: Government of India, Planning Commission: *Report of the committee of experts on unemployment estimates* (Dantwala Committee) (New Delhi, 1970), Appendix II, p. 53.

Table 45.   Activity status of urban population according to various rounds of the National Sample survey: four big cities, 1955-60, and West Bengal, 1960-67

NSS round	Period covered	No. in sample		Per cent of population			Unemploy- ed as % of labour force (4) : (5)	Source: NSS report	
		House- holds	Per- sons	Gain- fully employ- ed	Unem- ploy- ed	Labour force (3) + (4)		No.	Page
		(1)	(2)	(3)	(4)	(5)	(6)		
Four big cities [1] *(Stratum I):*									
9th	May 1955-Nov. 1955	3 164	14 788	35.37	2.94	38.31	7.67	62	117
10th	Dec. 1955-May 1956	3 022	13 716	36.67	3.56	40.23	8.45	34	155
11th 12th }	Aug. 1956-Aug. 1957	2 468	10 125	34.34	3.21	37.55	8.55	52	187
13th	Sep. 1957-Mar. 1958	2 121	8 908	33.75	2.87	36.62	7.84	63	150
14th	July 1958-June 1959	1 259	4 953	34.35	1.65	36.00	4.58	85	147
15th	July 1959-June 1960	1 252	5 186	34.68	2.41	37.09	6.50	157	112
West Bengal:									
16th	July 1960-June 1961	1 818	.	.	.	.	.	103	2
17th	Sep. 1961-July 1962	.	32 685	33.80	1.21	35.01	3.46	127	9
18th	Feb. 1963-Jan. 1964	.	9 376	35.99	0.98	36.97	2.65	152	14
19th	July 1964-June 1965	.	13 294	34.23	0.78	35.01	2.23	163	16
20th	July 1965-June 1966	.	9 519	34.17	0.70	34.87	2.01	166	14
21st	July 1966-June 1967	6 900	30 261	34.27	0.52	34.79	1.49	181	25

[1] Bombay, Calcutta, Delhi, Madras.

Source: *National Sample Survey* reports cited in body of table.

ANNEX B. URBAN INFRASTRUCTURE IN THE DEVELOPMENT
PLAN FOR THE CALCUTTA METROPOLITAN DISTRICT

The Calcutta Metropolitan Planning Organisation (CMPO) which was set up in 1961 owed its establishment partly to the international community's concern with the public health hazards arising from the desperate state of metropolitan Calcutta's water supply, sewerage and drainage. Following an unusually severe cholera epidemic in Calcutta in 1958, a World Health Organisation consultant team had examined in 1959 the environmental sanitation conditions of the Greater Calcutta area. As a result of their report, the U.N. Special Fund had financed in 1960 the preparation by a consortium of engineering firms of a master plan for metropolitan water supply, sewerage and drainage and, in the following year, the Government of West Bengal established the CMPO.

Also in 1960, a World Bank mission headed by Michael Hoffman had issued a report reviewing India's Third Five-Year Plan. The mission had devoted only a couple of pages of its report to Calcutta but had made a strong plea for the rehabilitation of the city.[1] Noting first that the failure to solve Calcutta's urban problems was putting impediments in the way of economic growth in what was then India's most rapidly expanding industrial region, the mission had then pointed out that the continued neglect of Calcutta's problems was one of the gravest weaknesses of the Third Plan. The mission had concluded its statement on Calcutta with a cautious endorsement of a Rs 2,000 million minimum programme of reconstruction of the city and a call for technical and financial assistance from abroad in such matters as land reclamation and urban planning.

In the event, technical assistance in urban planning was provided primarily by the Ford Foundation. The CMPO's basic development plan was published in 1966.[2] The plan, which was drawn up as a comprehensive framework for further social, economic and physical programming, included a description of Calcutta's urban infrastructure requirements. The description has been the basis for a number of sectoral plans: their main features are summarised below.

Water supply and drainage

Metropolitan Calcutta's water supply and drainage problem is at the heart of the city's physical crisis. The crisis had its beginnings two centuries ago when the main flow of the Ganges to the Bay of Bengal gradually shifted from its Bhagirathi-Hooghly arm, on which the East

---

[1] "Calcutta and the World Bank Mission", in *Economic Weekly* (Bombay), Vol. XII, No. 40, 1 Oct. 1960, pp. 1469-1474.

[2] See above, p. 1, n. 3.

India Company established its trading post in the 17th century, to its Padma arm in East Bengal. Progressive silting of the Bhagirathi has led to the current situation in which the normal flow of the Ganges enters the Bhagirathi-Hooghly channel only during the monsoon, with severe negative consequences both for Calcutta's water supply and drainage and for the city's port facilities.

With respect to water supply, the reduction in flow of fresh water has raised the salinity of the Hooghly to the point where pumping of river water into the city's main waterworks at Palta, 13 miles above Calcutta, must be interrupted at high tide during the three-month low flow period (April-June) before the monsoon because of encroachment of the tidal waters. By the late 1960s, the problem of high salinity at high tide in the pre-monsoon months could be kept under control only by holding raw water pumped from the Hooghly in the storage lagoon at Palta in order to deliver to Calcutta city water containing the average salinity over the period of a day or more.

At the same time, silting of the Hooghly in its lower reaches has progressively worsened the situation of Calcutta port. Sand bars and fluctuations in depth of flow in the 100 miles of river between the sea and Calcutta have greatly slowed ship movement to and from Calcutta port and have imposed a size limit of 10,000 tons (with draft of 26 feet) on ships entering the port. At the same time, silting of the lower Hooghly has caused a progressive raising of the river bed which in turn has intensified the severity of the bore tide, a rush of water resulting from the inflow of tidal water through a wide estuary when it reaches the river's shallower and narrower upstream channel. The bore tides have resulted in further silting up of the river and particularly of the riverside jetties and moorings in the Calcutta port.

The solution adopted to halt further deterioration of the river has been to redivert water from the Ganges to flush out the Hooghly by constructing a barrage at Farakka, above the point where the Ganges flows into Bangladesh, and a 25-mile feeder channel to the head of the Bhagirathi at Jangipur. The Farakka project was initiated in 1960/61 during India's Third Five-Year Plan; the barrage was scheduled for completion in 1972 and a railway line across the barrage was put into operation early in 1972. It will, however, be 1975 before the Hooghly channel is rehabilitated.

One of the several positive consequences for West Bengal and Calcutta of the separation of Bangladesh from Pakistan is that it de-fused the potential international conflict between India and East Pakistan that simmered for a decade over the future diversion of part of the Ganges flow at Farakka. In one of the first statements which the Prime Minister of Bangladesh made concerning Indo-Bangladesh relations during his visit to Calcutta on 6 February 1972, he specifically mentioned "co-operation between the two countries in the field of construction of barrages and flood control", while a joint statement issued in Calcutta on 8 February 1972 by the Prime Ministers of India and Bangladesh also referred to discussions of "the problem of flood control, the Farakka barrage and other problems of development of water and power resources".[1] In Article 6 of the first treaty of friendship, co-operation and peace signed in Dacca by the two prime ministers on 19 March 1972 it is declared that "the high contracting parties further agree to make joint studies and take further action in the fields of flood control, river basin development and the development of hydro-electric power and irrigation." The Indo-Bangladesh joint declaration signed on the same day specified that one of the decisions taken by the two prime ministers was "to establish a joint rivers commission comprising experts of both countries on a permanent basis to carry out a comprehensive survey of the river systems shared by the two countries, to formulate projects concerning both the countries in the field of flood control, and to implement them."[2]

The aims of the master plan are, by the year 2001, (a) to increase the supply of filtered water from a nominal 20 gallons a head per day to an effective and absolute 60 gallons/capita/day in Calcutta city and Howrah and 50 gallons/capita/day in the less populated

---

[1] *India and Foreign Review* (New Delhi), Vol. 9, No. 9, 15 Feb. 1972, p. 4.

[2] Ibid., Vol. 9, No. 12, 1 Apr. 1972, pp. 3-5.

Table 46. Estimated construction costs for water supply and drainage, master plan and
secondary works combined, 1966/67 - 2000/01, as of 1968
(Rs crores)

Item	Interim phase 1966/67 - 1970/71	Inter- mediate phase 1971/72 - 1980/81	Ultimate phase 1981/82 - 2000/01	Total
Water supply	11.87	76.67	61.02	149.56
Combined sewerage system	5.12	11.23	5.12	21.47
Separate sewerage and drainage	12.92	61.59	93.02	167.53
Outfall channels	0.20	0.70	1.10	2.00
Total	30.11	150.19	160.26	340.56

areas, while reducing the health hazards represented by untreated water first by treatment
and eventually by abolishing such supplies altogether, and (b) to provide a water-borne
sewerage system throughout the Calcutta Metropolitan District and a storm water drainage
system designed to reduce the incidence of flooding by three-quarters.

The proposed schemes for water supply are phased in time. Pending completion of the
diversionary channel from the Ganges at Farakka to the Bhagirathi-Hooghly, an "interim
water supply emergency scheme" would bring piped water from underground sources to all
urban areas within the Calcutta Metropolitan District. Ultimately groundwater sources will
supply the total demand at all times in the northern sector of the Calcutta Metropolitan
District (north of Palta and Serampore), while surface water supplies will replace all existing
or emergency groundwater supplies to the central and southern sectors wherever the population exceeds 25 persons per acre. The Calcutta Service District will be supplied by treated
Hooghly water from the existing plant at Palta and a new plant at Garden Reach. The
immediate target in terms of quantities of water supplied is to raise the minimum in the areas
which are both the worst provided and the most highly populated to 20 gallons/capita/day;
Howrah's current supply is 15 gallons/capita/day. By 1981, during the "intermediate phase"
of the programme, the minimum will be raised to 50 gallons/capita/day for Calcutta and
Howrah and to 40 gallons/capita/day for the other areas, on the way to the "ultimate phase"
target for 2001 mentioned above. In addition to providing extensions to the distribution
system, it will be necessary to repair or replace some of its existing elements, in particular
old steel piping in which there are many leaks.

The existing (Calcutta city, Titagarh, Serampore, Bhatpara, Kalyani[1]) or partly constructed (Manicktala[2], Dum Dum) sewerage systems in the Calcutta area are combined
sewerage and storm water drainage systems. Such combined systems have a number of
disadvantages, among them the health hazards arising from overflow of sewage with storm
waters during flood periods of the monsoon and the extra pumping needed during the seasons
of low water flow. In the northern sectors and in the city, the master plan calls for modification of the existing systems by the installation of overspill weirs in the sewers, construction
of new parallel drains and additional pumping facilities and the replacement or rehabilitation
of high-level conduits. In the southern suburban sector where a new system is still to be
installed, the master plan calls for an almost complete separation of sewerage and storm
drainage, with the storm drainage to be directed so as to discharge into Tolly's Nullah
and the Chetla boat canal, two surface waterways that cross the sector. Several natural lakes

[1] New town being developed near the east bank of the Hooghly opposite Bansberia.
[2] In the northern part of the city of Calcutta, to the south of Dum Dum.

in the southeast corner of the southern sector will be equipped with weirs and used as stabilising reservoirs. In areas close to the Hooghly, pumping facilities usable at high tide will be substituted for existing sluice gates usable only at low tide. The system will ultimately require up to 12 pumping stations, six of them as "priority undertakings".

An illustration of the importance of integrated physical planning of the various elements of urban infrastructure is the set of complications created for storm drainage by the implementation of two other "unrelated" projects: the filling-in of the Salt Lake swamp area to the east of Calcutta to create sites for housing; and the construction of a levee across a low-lying area off the eastern fringe of the residential and industrial suburbs north of Calcutta for the so-called VIP highway from Calcutta to Dum Dum international airport (the Dum Dum expressway). As a side effect both of these projects have upset the drainage pattern of the northern suburbs whose natural drainage flow is to the southeast, making the need for construction of an integrated drainage system even more urgent.

Transport

The rehabilitation and expansion of Calcutta's transport system is one of the more costly elements in the Metropolitan District's urban infrastructure programme since it includes such major undertakings as new bridges across the Hooghly river and construction of a new rapid mass transit system into central Calcutta. In addition, it includes the improvement, modernisation and expansion of the whole range of transport facilities: streets and highways, the existing mass transit systems, the external railway system, Calcutta port and the Calcutta airport at Dum Dum.

The basic development plan calls for the construction of three new bridges across the Hooghly: a high-level second Howrah bridge at Princep Ghat into the southern part of central Calcutta; a third Howrah bridge at Kalyani to link Kalyani and Bansberia at the northern end of the Calcutta Metropolitan District in the near term; and a fourth Howrah bridge into the northern part of central Calcutta some time in the 1980s. Improvement of the road transport system includes modernisation of the existing road system, construction of metropolitan access roads, construction of facilities to improve movement through the Metropolitan District and within central Calcutta, creation of trucking terminals, and provision for automobile parking.

The existing public mass transport system in the Calcutta area is close to saturation. The backbone of inner city public mass transport, the tramway system, is fully used and enormously overloaded. The number of buses, particularly those servicing the suburban areas, could be increased if foreign exchange availabilities were greater, but the roads leading into the inner city and the streets in the city can scarcely cope with the existing volume of traffic. The capacity of the suburban railway system is being adequately expanded by electrification and other modifications. Within the centre of the city, however, it seems unlikely that anything short of an underground (or overhead) rapid transit system will be able to cope with the rapidly increasing demand for public transport. The traffic and transportation plan[1] prepared by the CMPO with the assistance of consultants financed by the Ford Foundation and the World Bank and published in 1967 leaned rather heavily toward an overhead system at least for the initial north-south corridor from Dum Dum to Tollygunge. More recent plans have, however, fixed on an underground system.[2] The idea of a circular railway around Calcutta discussed in the basic development plan and in the traffic and transportation plan has been transformed into a suburban dispersal line whose possible implementation has been put off to the 1980s.[3]

---

[1] Calcutta Metropolitan Planning Organisation: *Traffic and transportation plan*, op. cit.

[2] Metropolitan Transport Project (Railways): *Calcutta mass transit study 1970-71: Dum Dum to Tollyganj* (Calcutta, 1971).

[3] Calcutta Metropolitan Planning Organisation, Traffic and Transportation Division: *Traffic study for the proposed rapid transit system and suburban dispersal line in Calcutta* (Calcutta, 1971).

Table 47. Estimated development costs for Calcutta Metropolitan District transportation plan proposals, 1966/67 - 1975/76, as of 1967
(Rs crores)

Item	1966/67 - 1970/71	1971/72 - 1975/76	1966/67 - 1975/76
Development of new street and highway facilities	47.47	33.51	80.98
Mass transportation [1]	2.60	43.20	45.80
Traffic engineering and area improvement plans	8.00	4.80	12.80
Parking	1.00	—	1.00
Major terminal facilities	0.50	1.00	1.50
Total	59.57	82.51	142.08

[1] Minimum requirements based on low-cost rapid transit system.

Source: CMPO: *Traffic and transportation plan for the Calcutta Metropolitan District 1966-1986* (Calcutta, 1967), p. 158.

Recent cost estimates for two major pieces of the proposed transport plan, the second Howrah bridge at Princep Ghat and the underground rapid transit line from Dum Dum to Tollygunge, come to Rs 1,700 million—Rs 300 million for the bridge and Rs 1,400 million for the underground.

The development of Calcutta's port will be directly affected by two of West Bengal's other major investment projects. One of them is the rehabilitation of the Hooghly on completion of the Farakka barrage and a new channel connecting the Ganges to the Bhagirathi, discussed above. The other is the construction of a deep-water bulk loading port on the Bay of Bengal at Haldia. The Haldia port will be able to handle cargo ships displacing up to 45,000 tons whereas the difficulties of navigating the Hooghly even after it is rehabilitated will limit access to Calcutta to ships displacing not more than 10,000 tons. The creation of Haldia port will stem the decline in the aggregate port activity of the Calcutta area; but it is not at all clear what it will do to the level and content of activity of Calcutta's existing port facilities. The handling of bulk cargo will clearly shift down river to Haldia, but it is precisely bulk cargo which is already being lost in relative and even in absolute terms to other more modern ports serving eastern India farther to the south. Calcutta's role as a distribution centre for smaller cargo is, however, not likely to be affected, while new activity on the river as it is made navigable up to Patna in Bihar is likely to expand the small-scale activities of Calcutta port.

Housing

The basic development plan wisely accepts as its basic premise the impossibility of providing adequate housing for all of metropolitan Calcutta's residents and places considerable weight, particularly for the short run, on improvement of the environmental conditions in Calcutta's bustee areas.[1] The housing plan therefore has three parts: bustee improvement and clearance; a limited amount of direct public housing construction; and encouragement to private housing construction by the provision of basic infrastructure and some financial incentives.

Bustee improvement

The Calcutta bustee is a collection of huts on land owned by a landlord but rented to an intermediary called the tikka tenant, who builds huts on the land and rents them out. A hut is legally defined in the Calcutta Municipal Act as a building "no substantial part

---

[1] See above, p. 86, n. 3.

of which, excluding the walls up to a height of 18 inches above the floor or floor level, is constructed of masonry, reinforced concrete, steel, iron or other metal". Over 900,000 people in metropolitan Calcutta, about a quarter of the total population of Calcutta city and a third of the population of Howrah Municipality and Bally, live in bustees.

At the time when the basic development plan was written, conditions in most of the bustees, some of which are probably as old as Calcutta itself, were appalling: incredibly over-crowded, insanitary, unlighted, unpaved, unsewered, without a safe water supply, provided, at best, with service privies, and flooded during the monsoon rains. The bustees are a locus of endemic cholera and have been the incubation centres for many epidemics. They nevertheless provide shelter, for which an alternative will be economically and physically impossible to provide for several decades to come. The basic development plan therefore places great stress on improvement of the immediate environment of the bustees: replacement of service privies by sanitary latrines, installation of a sanitary underground sewer system normally to be combined with storm drainage, provision of a supply of fresh water by tube wells and installation of community water taps and baths, pavement of pathways, installation of street lighting, and the treatment of the open ponds (tanks) where rain water for laundering and other purposes is collected and stored.

Bustee clearance runs into a number of legal and organisational problems of property rights and land use. In Calcutta all the bustees are on private lands, most of them held by tikka tenants. This is an exceptional situation in India: in Maharashtra, by contrast, 40 per cent of the shanty towns are on public lands. An earlier Slum Clearance and Improvement Act, which called for compensation at the rate of 60 times the monthly rental (i.e. five years' rent), has been a dead letter. Additional legislation is necessary in order to enter upon and improve private land without disturbing ownership patterns. The question whether the landlord (or the tikka tenant) would demand increased rents after improvements are made is still unanswered, although the odds are that the residents of the bustee would apply direct methods of persuasion if he did. The 25th Amendment to the Indian Constitution, which was enacted after the Supreme Court refused to sanction the Government of India's initial nationalisation of the commercial banks in 1969, deletes the notion of "compensation" for property taken over by the State for a public purpose and substitutes "an amount" to be paid according to certain principles to be decided upon. Housing can also be declared a public purpose. A special appeals tribunal will be set up to hear claims, which will not be justiciable in a court of law. It is envisaged that the State will take over bustee land, which will then either be used entirely for purposes other than housing or developed as split sites part of which would be for commercial use and part for housing. The slum dwellers in the city centre will eventually be moved, either elsewhere or to the housing portion of the split sites.

In 1967, the costs of physical improvement of the bustees were estimated at Rs 74.8 million for Calcutta and Rs 25.3 million for Howrah and Bally, using the factors of Rs 120 per capita for bustees in already sewered areas, Rs 150 per capita for bustees in totally unsewered areas, and Rs 140 in bustees adjacent to sewered areas.[1] These estimates are out of date.

Public housing construction

The volume of public housing to be included in the basic development plan was deliberately left unstated since it will depend primarily on the availability of financing. The expressed aims for the limited public housing programme are twofold: the first is to support public housing programmes already being carried out by existing and future agencies, to some extent by increasing the total number of units constructed but primarily by experimenting with new types of housing; the second is to provide a base for decent housing at a much

---

[1] CMPO: *Bustee improvement programme: Calcutta and Howrah* (Calcutta, October 1964, revised March 1967).

lower standard of construction than normal public housing, "to provide the maximum possible number of decent basic living accommodations rather than to produce housing of the highest quality".[1] This will be done first by installing the basic utility grid (streets, water, sewerage, drainage and lighting) and by supplying essential community services (education, health, garbage collection and adding, in the Indian context, community development and housing management), and secondly by choosing from a range of possibilities for assisting private persons in the construction of housing from light materials (kutcha housing).[2] The range covers: provision of a few building materials only; construction only of the plinth; provision of the basic structural frame; building of the entire kutcha house which could eventually be replaced by a house built from more permanent materials (pucca housing).[3] Open-plot development as such would involve provision of a pucca common lavatory and bath facility for each four or five plots. The CMPO broadens the open-plot concept by proposing the organised construction of temporary housing on an expanding ring of urban fringe land, eventually to be replaced by construction of permanent buildings for housing and for other purposes.

The principle of open-plot development for low income housing, which the World Bank is now calling "sites and services" development, is much debated in India. Experiments with open-plot development in Madras and in Delhi have been successful in attracting and holding residents, although in Delhi there has been some tendency for people relocated to the open-plot site to sell out their rights and move back into the inner city slums. The government housing authorities, however, object that the system is relatively expensive, particularly where land costs are high.

Private housing construction

Two major barriers to expansion of private housing construction noted in the basic development plan are the high cost of building materials, owing to nation-wide shortages, and the high cost of construction activity owing to the poor and antiquated organisation of the construction industry itself. A third is the shortage of financing for private construction.

A set of suggestions for encouraging private financing of housing construction has recently been elaborated by Kingsley and Kristof.[4] The target populations for the Kingsley-Kristof scheme would be the middle-class and lower-middle-class families. The proposals start from two basic assumptions, namely that medium-income and lower-medium-income families are willing to spend up to 15 per cent of household income for housing but usually spend less, and that the possibility of acquiring ownership of a dwelling by hire-purchase will provide the additional incentive needed for families to devote this proportion of their income to housing. On these assumptions, Kingsley and Kristof propose new designs which will lower housing costs, revised mortgage terms, a small government interest rate subsidy, and introduction of a hire-purchase plan for housing. Applied in combination, these should increase the effective market for middle-class housing by inducing consumers to devote to investment in housing, additional resources they would otherwise devote to other articles of consumption. At present costs better housing is beyond the reach of most middle-income households, who therefore devote as little as possible of their incomes to inadequate housing. If better housing were placed within reach by construction at somewhat lower cost (and quality) specifications and on easier financing terms, it is reasonable to predict that middle-class households would increase their budget allocation for housing at the expense of other items of consumption.

---

[1] CMPO: *Interim report: Housing, Calcutta Metropolitan District* (Calcutta, March 1967), p. 3.

[2] See above, p. 68, n. 3.

[3] See above, p. 68, n. 4.

[4] Kingsley and Kristof: *A housing policy for Metropolitan Calcutta*, op. cit.

Education and health

The CMPO's basic development plan included a set of physical targets for education and health infrastructure formulated in terms of the number of school places and hospital beds required for the Calcutta Metropolitan District.

Starting from the fact that in 1961 only 68 per cent of metropolitan Calcutta's children in the primary-school age group (6-10) and only 44 per cent of those in the junior-secondary age group (11-13) were school attendants, the CMPO accepted as an ultimate target for primary education the constitutional directive of free compulsory education for the age group 6-13 and as a more practical shorter-run goal the availability of primary education for all of the 6-10 age group. In its basic development plan, the CMPO proposed a target of 100 per cent coverage of the 6-10 age group by 1976, but with free education for only 50 per cent of that age group, to be increased to 100 per cent by 1986. School facilities would be built, where possible, as part of "community facility cores" where most needed—namely, in the new areas (Salt Lake, Kona[1], Sonarpur[2], Kalyani-Bansberia) and in the bustees. How to integrate school construction into bustee redevelopment was not discussed. The targets recommended for junior secondary education (ages 11-13) were 60 per cent enrolment by 1971, 75 per cent by 1976 and 100 per cent by 1986. Tentative targets for higher secondary education (ages 14-16) were put at 40 per cent for 1976 and 45 per cent for 1986, with the caveat that the establishment of precise targets and curricula required a full economic examination of manpower needs. It was recommended further that preference should be given to the suburban areas on both sides of the Hooghly as they were in serious deficit and sent their schoolchildren to the overcrowded facilities in central Calcutta. At the time of drafting of the basic development plan, over two-thirds of primary education pupils and a good part of junior secondary education pupils were educated at private institutions against payment of fees. Many of these private institutions, when they are officially recognised as meeting prescribed standards, receive public grants in aid. The shortage of recognised schools in relation to the demand for primary education has resulted in a mushrooming, especially in the bustees, of unrecognised schools whose teaching personnel exist without government subsidy on the low fees collected from the neighbourhood families whose children would otherwise go completely without formal schooling.

The targets for hospital beds were set on the standards of one bed per 1,000 population for the suburban areas of metropolitan Calcutta, and four beds per 1,000 population for Calcutta city. In addition, it will be necessary to develop neighbourhood clinics and health centres to relieve the strain on the hospitals.

These targets call for an increase in the total number of school places from 0.78 million in 1961 to 1.7 million in 1976 and 2.35 million in 1986 (see table 48). The number of hospital beds would increase from 14,000 in 1966 to 22,000 in 1986. At an average of 300 beds per hospital, this would imply an additional 27 hospitals for metropolitan Calcutta by 1986.

Implementation by the Calcutta Metropolitan Development Authority

The development programme for metropolitan Calcutta has been in a continuing state of revision and adjustment since the publication of the basic development plan in 1966, and even earlier. With the passage of time and the carrying out of further detailed studies, the scope of the programme has been expanded and the cost estimates for its implementation have been periodically revised upward. The cost of the programmes included in the basic development plan for 1966-1986 was estimated (presumably in 1965 prices) in the neighbourhood of Rs 150 crores, excluding railway electrification, modernisation of Calcutta

---

[1] Proposed new town in western part of Howrah planning area.

[2] Proposed new town south-east of Calcutta, north of Rajpur.

Table 48. Targets for school places and hospital beds, metropolitan Calcutta, 1961-1986
('000)

Category	1961	1966	1971	1976	1986
School places:					
Primary	510	.	755	1 044	1 318
Junior secondary	179	.	340	427	726
Higher secondary	89	.	176	229	305
Total	778	.	1 271	1 700	2 349
Hospital beds	.	14	18	19	22

Source: CMPO: *Basic development plan for the Calcutta Metropolitan District 1966-1986* (Calcutta, 1966), pp. 102, 103.

Table 49. Estimated cost of programmes in 1966-1986 basic development plan for Calcutta Metropolitan District, as of 1966
(Rs crores)

Category	Programmes in 1965 memorandum	Programmes not in 1965 memorandum	Total
Water supply	17.88	—	17.88
Sewerage and drainage	25.06	4.47	29.53
Environmental hygiene	4.00	—	4.00
Traffic and transportation [1]	48.96	11.83	60.79
Special projects [2]	3.31	—	3.31
Housing and new area development	19.85	—	19.85
Subtotal	119.06	16.30	135.36
CMPO expenses	1.50	—	1.50
Land acquisition for bustee improvement	15.00	—	15.00
Total	135.56	16.30	151.86

[1] Excluding railway electrification, modernisation of Calcutta port, and improvement of Calcutta airport (included in other budgets). [2] Urban community development; Calcutta gas system.

Source: CMPO: *Basic development plan for the Calcutta Metropolitan District 1966-1986*, op. cit., pp. 143-155 and Table 39 (pp. 158-165).

port and improvement of Calcutta airport, whose costs would be borne by the other budgets of the Railway Ministry, the Port Commissioners and the Ministry of Civil Aviation (see table 49). The cost estimates for an expanded water supply and drainage programme were substantially increased as a result of the work of the UNDP/WHO team on the master plan (see table 46). Tentative estimates of the costs of a traffic and transport programme extending over the period 1966/67-1975/76 were established in 1967 by the CMPO's traffic and transportation team and its associated consultants (see table 47) and are also being revised upward as plans for major projects such as an underground rapid transit system become firmer. The total cost of the working programme for urban development was estimated as of January 1972 at Rs 221 crores, not including provision for construction of the underground railway (see table 50).

Table 50. Estimated cost of development programme for metropolitan Calcutta, as of January 1972
      (Rs crores)

Item	Estimated total cost	Fourth Plan provision (1969/70 - 1973/74)	Anticipated expenditure level 1971/72
Water supply	50.91	32.21	6.81
Sewerage and drainage	70.54	39.74	11.53
Garbage disposal	4.00	2.28	1.55
Environmental hygiene	4.67	1.65	0.33
Traffic and transportation [1]	64.55	36.49	12.63
Special projects	10.26	15.29	2.45
Housing and new area development	6.53	30.91	3.21
Subtotal	211.47	158.56	38.51
Organisational expenses:			
CMPO	—	—	0.35
CMDA	—	—	0.59
Purchase of scarce materials [2]	—	—	5.00
Bustee improvement scheme	9.83	10.00	5.06
Total	221.30	168.56	49.51

[1] Excludes mass transportation rapid transit system.   [2] Cement, asphalt, steel, vehicles.

Source: CMDA: *1971-1972 plan programme, Expenditure progress as on 31 December 1971, Statement No. 6, Effective date: 17 January 1972* (Calcutta, mimeographed).

Although the basic development plan was published in 1966, its active implementation got under way only at the end of 1970, after the creation of the Calcutta Metropolitan Development Authority (CMDA) and the allocation of central Government funds directly to the CMDA.[1] The Government of India, which was then directly responsible for West Bengal under President's rule, authorised an outlay of Rs 150 crores for metropolitan Calcutta for the remaining three years (1971/72 - 1973/74) of the Fourth Plan period, or approximately Rs 50 crores annually. Approximately this rate of annual expenditure was reached in 1971/72 (see table 50). The programme covers, in particular, water supply, sewerage and drainage, traffic and transportation, housing development and slum clearance and improvement, and special projects. As indicated in table 50, the figure of Rs 150 crores has been adjusted upward.

As of the beginning of Indian fiscal year 1972/73, financing was more or less assured for about Rs 120 crores, as shown below:

                                                  Rs crores

	Rs crores
Fourth Plan allocation for Calcutta	43
Market borrowing	30
Octroi (goods entry tax)	20
Central Government grant for bustee improvement	8
Special central Government loan (4 × Rs 5 crores)	20
	121

Authorising the CMDA to levy a tax on goods entering metropolitan Calcutta was an unusual step for the central Government to take.

[1] See above, p. 65.

In its first year of operation, the CMDA concentrated its energies and its publicity on programmes which would have an immediate and direct effect on living conditions in Calcutta. Particular stress was laid on visible earth-moving operations: installation of sewer and storm drains in several major bustee areas; road repair and improvement; reconstruction of the Howrah station plaza; clearance of major storm water channels close in to Calcutta city (Tolly's Nullah, Circular Canal, and others); and immediate improvements in the garbage collection system. The flurry of activity had a positive physical and psychological impact on Calcutta. For the first time in a number of years, there appeared to be hope that the city could be pulled out of the morass into which it had been sinking.

Part of the immediate success of the programme once it got moving is due to the fact that the CMDA's operations are projects sponsored by the central Government after approval by a permanent review body of the Government of India. There is no requirement for approval by the West Bengal State Finance Ministry, although the latter is consulted during their formulation.

Continuation of CMDA's initial momentum will depend in part on the extent to which public housing construction can be stepped up. Over the last 20 years, about 25,000 housing units per year were built, as compared with a need reckoned at 37,000 just to keep up with the population increase.[1] Of these, 3,000 per year were built by the public housing authorities—a rate which it is now intended to step up to 12,000 per year. An alternative is to give out on contract the construction of perhaps 10,000 units to architect-builder firms on a turn-key basis.

The major area for new housing in metropolitan Calcutta is the former Salt Lake which was filled in, at the cost of Rs 20 crores per five square miles, with silt pumped from the Hooghly. Streets, lighting and sewerage have been prepared for three square miles, and 5,000 plots of varying sizes have been put out to sale. On 3,000 plots already allotted, only 100 houses had been built by early 1972. The main development will have to be carried out under public housing projects.

At present there is a housing directorate which is the construction and maintenance agent for the housing activities of the West Bengal State Government. A proposal for a new housing board for West Bengal is under consideration. Two decisions have still to be taken: whether or not to include Calcutta within the new housing board's jurisdiction, and the nature of the relationship of the housing board to the CMDA if Calcutta is included.

Another organisation working in the housing field in Calcutta is the central Government's Housing and Urban Development Corporation (HUDCO), which has a Rs 200 crore fund at its disposal for the financing of slum clearance and the development of commercial premises and housing on commercial terms throughout India. In other states, HUDCO finances local agencies; in Calcutta, HUDCO is directly involved in the purchase of land and in construction activity, with the CMDA co-opted as the overseeing authority. HUDCO has already purchased (for Rs 2 million) four acres out of a 17-acre tract in Calcutta and is negotiating the purchase of the Calcutta golf course. Of the all-India total of Rs 200 crores, Rs 20 crores have already been committed and it is expected that Rs 80 crores will be committed by the end of the Fourth Five-Year Plan (March 1974). HUDCO is conceived as a financing body which intends to conserve and to increase its initial capital. It lends at 1.5 per cent above the bank rate with a state government guarantee of the loan, or at 7.5 per cent against collateral but without a state government guarantee. Loans are repayable in 6-10 years. HUDCO can therefore take up housing for upper-middle-income families (those with above Rs 1,000 per month) who can amortise housing units costing Rs 40,000. In Calcutta, HUDCO plans to construct 500 such units.

For upper-middle-income groups, housing can probably be encouraged in the short run by an interest subsidy. In a few years' time, the private land market will pick up and produce adequate housing for such groups, who can amortise housing in 15-25 years by allocating to it 20-25 per cent of current income.

---

[1] Kingsley and Kristof: *A housing policy for metropolitan Calcutta*, op. cit., p. I-1.

The CMDA considers that, in the housing field, its concern should be the households receiving less than Rs 1,000 per month. Even with an income between Rs 400 and Rs 1,200 per month, a household cannot amortise a proper dwelling unit. For the two-thirds of the households in metropolitan Calcutta who receive less than Rs 400, the Kingsley-Kristof suggestions for building new economy settlements at very low cost, combined with continued slum improvement and modernisation, would provide a solution provided that sufficient funds were available, which unfortunately is not the case.

Of the CMDA programme of more than Rs 150 crore for the last three years of the Fourth Five-Year Plan, Rs 10 crores have been earmarked for bustee improvement and another Rs 10 crores for bustee acquisition, clearance and redevelopment. Owing to the intensity of the current housing shortage in Calcutta, slum clearance is for the time being out of the question and efforts are being concentrated on improving the quality of life in the bustees by installing piped water (at standpipes rather than directly in dwelling units), water-operated privies, sewer connections, paved streets and street lighting.

In the field of transport the north-south Dum Dum-Tollygunge line of the proposed Calcutta underground rapid transit system has been cleared by the Planning Commission and the Government of India. The central railway budget for 1972/73 contained a Rs 6 million item for further detailed design work on the underground.

A transport project which has recently been revived is a Rs 3.5 crore road bridge across the Hooghly at Kalyani, at the northern end of the Calcutta Metropolitan District. The bridge will facilitate access from the west to Jessore in Bangladesh. Some outlay on preliminary work for the bridge is included in the 1972/73 budget.

ANNEX C. INCOME AND EXPENDITURE DATA FROM THE HINDUSTAN THOMPSON STUDY OF FOOD HABITS IN CALCUTTA

The most recent source of household income and expenditure data for Calcutta is the survey carried out in 1969/70 by the Research Department of Hindustan Thompson Associates in Calcutta for the Protein Food Association of India and the Nutrition Branch of the United States Agency for International Development Mission to India in New Delhi.[1]

The pattern of consumption by per capita income level that emerges from the study calls for two preliminary interpretative remarks. The first is that the investigators asked the persons being interviewed two independent questions or sets of questions relating to consumption levels: one relating to their estimate of total expenditure and the other relating to the detailed components of household expenditure. The investigators were specifically instructed not to ask the respondent to reconcile the global estimate with the sum of the details. The questionnaires were sorted according to the respondent's global expenditure estimate, which in most cases turned out to be below the sum of the detailed components of household expenditure. Consequently, the average income for all the per capita income classes below Rs 200 per month lies outside (above) the reported income class. This oddity is, however, of no consequence for the analysis of consumption changes since all calculations refer to the average income entry for the class rather than to the class range.

The second remark is to note that what is here called "income", the report calls total household expenditure including saving and debt repayment. The present writer's interpretation of saving as the difference between total consumption and income may be unwarranted. As it happens, the progression of saving with rising total income is somewhat erratic; saving shows a particularly peculiar fall from the second highest income category (Rs 301-400) to the highest (Rs 401 and over), instead of the expected rise.

The Hindustan Thompson Associates study covered a sample of almost 15,000 persons in Calcutta city. The report gives an interesting tabulation of the distribution of the sample population by occupation and by income group (see table 51). The distribution of employed persons in the sample (that is, excluding students, housewives and "others") by occupation was as follows (in per cent):

Unskilled manual workers	28.4	Professionals	7.8
Skilled manual workers	17.2	Businessmen	5.1
Small traders	13.0	Landlords, pensioners, *rentiers*	4.1
Clerical workers	15.7	Other employed persons	5.1
Officers	3.6	**Total**	**100.0**

---

[1] Hindustan Thompson Associates Ltd.: *A study of food habits in Calcutta,* op. cit. See above, p. 72.

(text continued on p. 132)

Table 51. Distribution of persons by occupation and by income group in Calcutta, 1969/70.

In percentages

Monthly income (Rs) / Occupation	(1) No income	(2) ≤ 75	(3) 76-150	(4) 151-300	(5) 301-500	(6) 501-750	(7) 751-1 000	(8) 1 001-1 500	(9) 1 501-2 000	(10) > 2 000	(11) Income unknown	(12) All [1]	(13) All employed [2]
Unskilled manual workers	—	6.10	2.02	0.71	0.06	0.01	—	—	—	—	—	9.09	28.39
Skilled manual workers	—	0.83	2.47	1.52	0.42	0.05	0.01	—	—	—	0.20	5.51	17.21
Small traders	—	0.42	0.95	1.37	0.56	0.13	0.06	0.01	—	0.01	0.65	4.15	12.96
Clerical workers	—	0.11	0.81	1.88	1.62	0.28	0.08	0.02	0.01	—	0.21	5.02	15.68
Officers	—	—	0.02	0.07	0.20	0.38	0.26	0.09	0.04	0.04	0.03	1.14	3.56
Professionals	—	0.17	0.30	0.71	0.52	0.30	0.19	0.13	0.05	0.04	0.11	2.51	7.84
Businessmen	—	0.01	0.06	0.15	0.32	0.24	0.21	0.22	0.05	0.07	0.32	1.65	5.15
Landlords, pensioners, rentiers	—	0.14	0.27	0.29	0.13	0.03	0.04	0.01	0.03	0.01	0.36	1.32	4.12
Students	28.29	0.11	0.02	—	0.01	—	—	—	—	0.01	0.01	28.44	·
Housewives	19.16	0.13	0.03	0.07	0.01	0.04	0.02	—	0.01	0.01	0.01	19.50	·
Employed persons not enumerated above	—	0.42	0.40	0.24	0.17	0.05	0.02	0.01	—	—	0.34	1.63	5.09
Others	19.63	0.10	0.09	0.03	—	—	0.01	—	0.01	—	0.17	20.03	·
Total	67.08	8.56	7.42	7.03	4.02	1.52	0.90	0.48	0.19	0.19	2.62	100.00	100.00
Number of persons in sample	9 978	1 273	1 104	1 045	598	226	134	71	28	29	389	14 875	·

[1] Rounding as in original. [2] Excluding students, housewifes and residual "others" category.

Source: Hindustan Thompson Associates Ltd.: A study of food habits in Calcutta, op. cit., Table A21.

Table 52. Distribution of persons by income group within occupations in Calcutta, 1969/70

In percentages

Monthly income (Rs) — Occupation	(1) No income	(2) ≤ 75	(3) 76-150	(4) 151-300	(5) 301-500	(6) 501-750	(7) 751-1 000	(8) 1 001-1 500	(9) 1 501-2 000	(10) > 2 000	(11) Income unknown	(12) All
Unskilled manual workers	—	67.11	22.22	7.81	0.66	97.91	—	—	—	—	—	100.00
Skilled manual workers	—	15.06	44.83	27.59	7.62	0.91	0.18	—	—	—	0.18	100.00
Small traders	—	10.12	22.89	33.01	13.49	3.13	1.44	0.24	—	0.24	15.66	100.00
Clerical workers	—	2.19	16.14	37.45	32.27	5.58	1.59	0.40	0.20	—	4.18	100.00
Officers	—	—	1.75	6.14	17.54	33.33	22.81	7.89	3.51	3.51	2.63	100.00
Professionals	—	6.77	11.95	28.29	20.72	11.95	7.57	5.18	1.99	1.59	4.38	100.00
Businessmen	—	0.61	3.64	9.09	19.39	14.54	12.73	13.33	3.03	4.24	19.39	100.00
Landlords, pensioners, *rentiers*	—	10.61	20.45	21.97	9.85	2.27	3.03	0.76	2.27	0.76	27.27	100.00
Students	99.47	0.39	0.07	0.03	0.03	—	—	—	—	0.03	0.03	100.00
Housewives	98.26	0.67	0.15	0.36	0.05	0.20	0.10	—	0.05	0.05	0.05	100.00
Employed persons not enumerated above	—	25.77	24.54	14.72	10.43	3.07	1.23	0.61	—	—	20.86	100.00
Others	98.00	0.50	0.45	0.15	—	—	0.05	—	0.05	—	0.85	100.00
Whole sample	67.08	8.56	7.42	7.03	4.02	1.52	0.90	0.48	0.19	0.19	2.62	100.00

Source: Derived from table 51.

Table 53. Consumer expenditure by monthly income per capita and commodity category, Calcutta, 1969/70

In rupees

Per capita monthly income class as estimated by respondents (Rs) / Item	(1) ≤ 15	(2) 16 -20	(3) 21 -30	(4) 31 -40	(5) 41 -60	(6) 61 -80	(7) 81 -100	(8) 101 -125	(9) 126 -150	(10) 151 -175	(11) 176 -200	(12) 201 -250	(13) 251 -300	(14) 301 -40	(15) > 401	(16) All
Income	31.57	39.38	45.86	57.66	77.61	98.69	127.16	155.87	161.61	199.67	209.65	223.83	255.13	303.25	425.23	98.48
Saving	0.02	0.04	0.10	0.28	0.69	2.22	3.30	4.38	7.19	10.45	10.19	17.19	12.54	28.04	18.94	2.76
Consumption (total)	31.55	39.34	45.76	57.38	76.92	96.47	123.86	151.49	154.42	189.22	199.46	206.64	242.59	275.21	406.29	95.72
Food	21.66	26.08	29.55	36.13	45.14	54.72	61.18	69.33	69.69	80.62	88.88	90.76	104.46	113.74	127.05	49.88
Non-food	9.89	13.26	16.21	21.25	31.78	41.75	62.68	82.16	84.73	108.60	110.58	115.88	138.13	161.47	279.24	45.84
Tobacco	0.66	0.87	0.82	1.09	1.32	1.78	2.01	2.29	2.87	3.91	2.63	3.75	3.84	4.12	5.13	1.64
Fuel and light	1.18	1.64	1.80	2.22	3.08	3.64	4.38	5.09	6.06	7.64	7.38	8.64	8.64	8.79	14.37	3.61
Clothing, bedding, etc.	1.81	1.73	2.22	2.74	3.86	4.79	7.30	9.15	9.32	12.04	12.51	11.42	17.11	10.29	34.58	5.33
Miscellaneous goods and services	3.50	5.31	6.84	9.26	14.22	19.70	29.51	40.03	35.50	46.13	49.42	50.44	63.85	73.41	119.81	20.59
Durable and semi-durable goods	0.58	0.97	1.06	1.65	3.07	3.03	7.06	8.90	10.49	11.45	8.76	11.87	12.60	20.12	33.02	4.67
Rent and taxes	1.89	2.44	2.63	3.27	4.43	6.09	8.78	10.84	14.48	20.62	19.37	21.54	24.80	31.78	40.68	7.15
Other expenses	0.24	0.30	0.55	0.60	0.78	1.29	1.37	1.93	2.14	3.47	4.63	6.20	5.35	8.19	5.75	1.35
Remittances made	0.13	—	0.29	0.42	1.02	1.43	2.27	3.93	3.87	3.34	5.88	2.02	1.94	4.77	5.90	1.50
Number of persons in sample	655	822	1 811	2 247	3 099	1 769	1 645	731	649	307	423	243	184	149	141	14 875

Source: *A study of food habits in Calcutta*, op. cit., table A54, pp. 62-65.

Table 54. Percentage distribution of expenditure within individual income brackets, Calcutta, 1969/70

Item / Per capita monthly income class as estimated by respondents (Rs)	(1) ≤15	(2) 16-20	(3) 21-30	(4) 31-40	(5) 41-60	(6) 61-80	(7) 81-100	(8) 101-125	(9) 126-150	(10) 151-175	(11) 176-200	(12) 201-250	(13) 251-300	(14) 301-400	(15) >401	(16) All
Income	100.00	100.00	100.00	100.00	100.00	100.00	100.00	100.00	100.00	100.00	100.00	100.00	100.00	100.00	100.00	100.00
Saving	0.06	0.10	0.22	0.49	0.89	2.25	2.60	2.81	4.45	5.23	4.86	7.68	4.92	9.25	4.40	2.80
Consumption (total)	99.04	99.90	99.78	99.51	99.11	97.75	97.40	97.19	95.55	94.77	95.14	92.32	95.08	90.75	95.54	97.20
Food	68.61	66.23	64.44	62.66	58.16	55.44	48.11	44.48	43.12	40.38	42.39	40.55	40.94	37.51	29.88	50.65
Non-food	30.43	33.67	35.34	36.85	40.95	42.31	49.29	52.71	52.43	54.39	52.75	51.77	54.14	53.24	65.66	46.55
Tobacco	1.77	2.21	1.79	1.89	1.70	1.80	1.58	1.47	1.78	1.96	1.25	1.67	1.51	1.36	1.21	1.67
Fuel and light	3.74	4.16	3.92	3.85	3.97	3.69	3.45	3.26	3.75	3.83	3.52	3.86	3.39	2.90	3.38	3.66
Clothing, bedding, etc.	5.74	4.39	4.84	4.75	4.97	4.85	5.74	5.87	5.77	6.03	5.97	5.10	6.71	3.40	3.13	5.41
Miscellaneous goods and services	11.08	13.48	14.91	16.06	18.32	19.97	23.21	25.68	21.96	23.10	23.58	22.54	25.02	24.20	28.17	20.92
Durable and semi-durable goods	1.84	2.47	2.31	2.86	3.96	3.07	5.54	5.72	6.49	5.73	4.18	5.31	4.93	6.63	12.46	4.71
Rent and taxes	5.99	6.20	5.74	5.67	5.71	6.17	6.90	6.95	8.96	10.33	9.24	9.62	9.72	10.48	9.57	7.26
Other expenses	0.76	0.76	1.20	1.04	1.01	1.31	1.08	1.24	1.32	1.74	2.21	2.77	2.10	2.70	1.35	1.37
Remittances made	0.41	—	0.63	0.73	1.31	1.45	1.79	2.52	2.40	1.67	2.80	0.90	0.76	1.57	1.39	1.52
Percentage of persons in sample	*4.41*	*5.53*	*12.17*	*15.11*	*20.84*	*11.89*	*11.06*	*4.91*	*4.36*	*2.06*	*2.84*	*1.63*	*1.24*	*1.00*	*0.95*	*100.00*

Source: *A study of food habits in Calcutta*, op. cit., table A55, pp. 66-69.

Table 55. Percentage distribution of income and consumption per capita, by income bracket, Calcutta, 1969/70

Per capita monthly income class as estimated by respondents (Rs) / Item	(1) ≤ 15	(2) 16 -20	(3) 21 -30	(4) 31 -40	(5) 41 -60	(6) 61 -80	(7) 81 -100	(8) 101 -125	(9) 126 -150	(10) 151 -175	(11) 176 -200	(12) 201 -250	(13) 251 -300	(14) 301 -400	(15) > 400	(16) All
A. In individual income brackets:																
Sample persons	4.41	5.53	12.17	15.11	20.84	11.89	11.06	4.91	4.36	2.06	2.84	1.63	1.24	1.00	0.95	100.00
Total income	1.40	2.20	5.67	8.84	16.42	11.92	14.28	7.78	7.16	4.19	6.05	3.71	3.21	3.08	4.09	100.00
Total consumption	1.45	2.27	5.82	9.05	16.74	11.98	14.31	7.78	7.04	4.08	5.92	3.53	3.13	2.88	4.02	100.00
B. Cumulative:[1]																
Sample persons	4.41	9.94	22.11	37.22	58.06	69.95	81.01	85.92	90.28	92.34	95.18	96.81	98.05	99.05	100.00	.
Total income	1.40	3.60	9.27	18.11	34.53	46.45	60.73	68.51	75.67	79.86	85.91	89.62	92.83	95.91	100.00	.
Total consumption	1.45	3.72	9.54	18.59	35.33	47.31	61.62	69.40	76.44	80.52	86.44	89.97	93.10	95.98	100.00	.

[1] These distributions are charted by the Lorenz curves shown in the figure on page 131. The Gini coefficient of inequality (the area between the 45° line and the Lorenz curve in the figure divided by the total area under the 45° line) is 0.312 for income and 0.301 for consumption.

Source: Derived from table 53.

Figure. Lorenz curves for per capita income and expenditure, Calcutta, 1969/70
(Cumulative percentages)

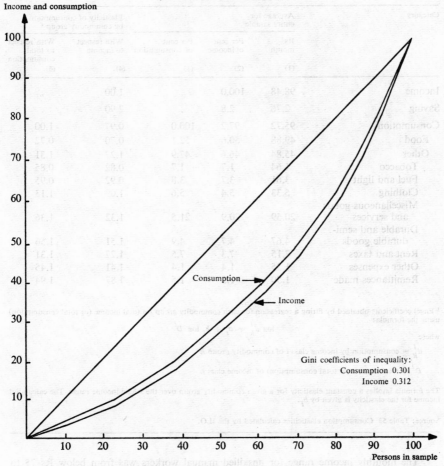

Income and consumption

Consumption

Income

Gini coefficients of inequality:
Consumption 0.301
Income 0.312

Persons in sample

These constant elasticity estimates were obtained by fitting to the rupee data in table 53 regression equations of the form:

$$\log d^i_k = a_i + b_i \log D^i$$

where:

d^i_k = consumption by income class i of commodity group k;

D^i = total income (or total consumption) of income class i.

The calculated parameter b_i in the equation is the elasticity. For the Calcutta data, in all cases except that of "remittances made" the equation fits the data very closely (with correlation coefficients of 0.99 or over).

An alternative formulation, which yields variable elasticities, is to fit regression equations of the form:

$$\log d^i_k = a'_i + b'_i \log D^i + c (\log D^i)^2.$$

In this formulation, elasticity is increasing if c_i is positive, decreasing if c_i is negative, and constant if $c_i = 0$.

The value of the elasticity at any specific value of D^i is given by:

$$b_i + 2 C_i (\log D^i).$$

131

Table 56. Average per capita income and consumption, and elasticities of consumption, by commodity groups, Calcutta, 1969/70

Category	Average for entire sample			Elasticity of consumption by commodity group [1]	
	Rs/ month	Per cent of income	Per cent of consumption	With respect to income	With respect to total consumption
	(1)	(2)	(3)	(4)	(5)
Income	98.48	100.0	.	1.00	.
Saving	2.76	2.8	.	2.90	.
Consumption	95.72	97.2	100.0	0.97	1.00
Food	49.88	50.6	52.1	0.70	0.72
Other	45.84	46.6	47.9	1.27	1.31
Tobacco	1.64	1.7	1.7	0.82	0.85
Fuel and light	3.61	3.7	3.8	0.92	0.95
Clothing	5.33	5.4	5.6	1.09	1.13
Miscellaneous goods and services	20.59	20.9	21.5	1.32	1.36
Durable and semi-durable goods	4.67	4.7	4.9	1.51	1.56
Rent and taxes	7.15	7.3	7.5	1.27	1.31
Other expenses	1.35	1.4	1.4	1.41	1.45
Remittances made	1.50	1.5	1.5	1.87	1.94

[1] Engel coefficients obtained by fitting a regression for each commodity group on total income (or total consumption) using the formula:

$$\log d_k^i = a_i + b_i \log D^i$$

where

d_k^i = consumption by income class i of commodity group k

D^i = total income (or total consumption) of income class i.

The formula implies a constant elasticity for a given commodity group over the whole income range. The calculated income for the elasticity is given by b_i.

Source: Table 53. Consumption elasticities calculated by the ILO.

The monthly income range for unskilled manual workers was from below Rs 75 to Rs 750 with 67 per cent of them concentrated in the Rs 1-75 group (see table 52). Among skilled manual workers, a few were to be found in the Rs 751-1,000 group, while the heaviest concentration, 45 per cent, were in the Rs 76-150 group. The incomes of small traders ranged up to over Rs 2,000, but the distribution showed a peak (with 33 per cent) in the Rs 151-300 group. Clerical workers are concentrated in the Rs 151-300 group (37 per cent) and in the Rs 301-500 group (32 per cent), as are professionals (28 per cent in Rs 151-300 and 21 per cent in Rs 301-500). Businessmen show the highest concentrations (20 per cent) in the Rs 301-500 and in the "income unknown" groups but are also fairly evenly spread over the next three higher groups, Rs 501-750, Rs 751-1,000, and Rs 1,001-1,500.

A general description of the inequality of income distribution of all persons within the Hindustan Thompson sample is given by the two Lorenz curves, for income and consumption, shown in the figure, page 131. The Gini coefficient of inequality is 0.312 for income, and 0.301 for consumption (see table 55).

A summary of the data on the pattern of consumption by per capita income level presented in table 53 distinguishes two major consumption groups, food and non-food, within total consumption and the following eight categories within the non-food group:

Table 57. Variable elasticities of consumption for selected categories of household expenditure[1], Calcutta, 1969/70

Category \ Per capita income (Rs)	Variable elasticity at selected income levels					Constant elasticity[2]
	30	50	100	200	400	
With respect to income:						
Food	0.84	0.78	0.71	0.63	0.56	0.70
Miscellaneous goods and services	1.62	1.50	1.34	1.18	1.02	1.32
Remittances made	4.13	3.24	2.03	0.83	− 0.37	1.87
With respect to total consumption:						
Food	0.87	0.81	0.73	0.64	0.56	0.72
Miscellaneous goods and services	1.66	1.54	1.38	1.22	1.05	1.36
Remittances made	4.19	3.28	2.05	0.81	− 0.42	1.94

[1] Engel coefficients obtained by fitting a regression for each commodity group on total income or total consumption using the formula:

$$\log d_k^i = a'_i + b'_i \log D^i + c_i (\log D^i)^2$$

where:

d_k^i = consumption by income class i of commodity group k

D^i = total income (or total consumption) of income class i.

The elasticity is increasing when $c_i > 0$, decreasing when $c_i < 0$, and constant when $c_i = 0$. The calculated value of the elasticity for a specific income level is given by $b'_i + 2c_i (\log D^i)$.

[2] Table 56, col. 4.

Source: Table 53. Consumption elasticities calculated by the ILO.

tobacco; fuel and light; clothing; miscellaneous goods and services; durable and semi-durable goods and services; rent and taxes; other expenses; remittances made.

In the lowest income category, food expenditure accounts for nearly 69 per cent of total income, but the proportion devoted to food is markedly lower at higher income levels (see table 54). All the other kinds of expenditure tend to increase as a proportion of total income as incomes rise. The item whose share shows the fastest rise at the lower income levels is remittances made. It should be noted, however, that remittances reach a maximum share of only 2.8 per cent, at a per capita income level of Rs 176-200 per month.[1]

The average pattern for all persons in the sample (whose average income was Rs 98.48 per month) shows saving at only 2.8 per cent of total income, food consumption at 50.7 per cent and non-food consumption at 46.6 per cent. The miscellaneous goods and services category within non-food absorbed 20.9 per cent. Rent and taxes absorbed 7.3 per cent, a much lower figure than the 15 per cent target for housing cited in the Kingsley-Kristof report on housing construction.[2] Remittances made by the whole sample population absorbed 1.5 per cent of income.

The most useful indicator of the change in consumption patterns from the lower to the higher income levels is the elasticity of consumption of a given commodity group, the elasticity being defined as the proportional change in consumption divided by the proportional change in income. Constant Engel coefficients (elasticities of consumption) calculated

[1] The entries for per capita income classes Rs 176-200 and Rs 201-250 in tables 54 and 55 seem out of line with respect to both savings and remittances.

[2] Kingsley and Kristof: *A housing policy for Metropolitan Calcutta*, op. cit. See Annex B above, p. 119.

Table 58. Per capita monthly income and food expenditure, cereals and other, Calcutta, 1969/70

Category / Per capita income estimated by respondents (Rs)	≤ 20	21-40	41-60	61-100	> 100	Average
From total expenditure table:			*(rupees)*			
Income	35.91	52.39	77.61	112.41	203.50	98.48
Total consumption	35.88	52.19	76.92	109.67	193.34	95.72
Food	24.12	33.19	45.14	57.83	83.07	49.88
From food expenditure table: [1]						
Total food	23.90	32.86	44.64	57.13	80.66	48.92
Cereals	11.00	13.18	15.13	14.04	13.86	13.39
Other	12.90	19.68	30.75	43.09	66.80	13.39
Cereals consumption as proportion of—			*(per cent)*			
Income	30.63	25.16	19.49	12.49	6.8	13.60
Total consumption	30.66	25.25	19.67	12.80	7.2	13.99
Food consumption:						
Total expenditure table	45.60	39.71	33.52	24.28	16.68	26.84
Food expenditure table	46.02	40.11	33.89	24.58	17.18	27.37
Elasticity of cereals consumption with respect to—			*(ratio)*			
Income	.	0.43	0.31	−0.16	−0.02	.
Total consumption	.	0.44	0.31	−0.17	−0.02	.

[1] Daily consumption multiplied by 31.

Source: Derived from *A study of food habits in Calcutta*, op. cit., table A37, p. 41, and table A54, pp. 62-65.

for the ten individual categories of expenditure (table 56) show an elasticity of 0.7 for food consumption and close to 1.3 for non-food consumption. In other words, each 1.0 per cent rise in income results in a 0.7 per cent rise in food consumption and a 1.3 per cent rise in non-food consumption. Within non-food consumption, the elasticities show an interesting (and expected) progression: 0.8 for tobacco, 0.9 for fuel and light, 1.1 for clothing, 1.3 for miscellaneous goods and services, 1.5 for durable and semi-durable goods, 1.3 for rent and taxes, 1.4 for other expenses, and 1.9 for remittances made.

The variable elasticities calculated from these consumption data are statistically significant for only three of the commodity groups: food; miscellaneous goods and services; and remittances made. Each of these shows declining elasticities with rising income (see table 57). For food consumption the variable elasticity calculation shows an elasticity of 0.8 at a low income level, declining to 0.6 at the highest income levels; at the average monthly income of Rs 100, the variable elasticity coefficient is close to the constant elasticity coefficient, 0.7. For miscellaneous goods and services, the variable elasticity declines from 1.6 at a low income level to 1.0 at the highest income level, and is also, at 1.3, close to the constant elasticity coefficient at the average monthly income of Rs 100. For remittances made, the variable elasticity declines from 4.1 at the lower end of the income range to −0.4 at the upper end; at the Rs 100 monthly income level it is 2.1, a little above the constant elasticity coefficient of 1.9.

It would be interesting to obtain corresponding elasticities for the consumption of cereals. Unfortunately, the study tabulates food consumption expenditure in great detail

Table 59. Consumer expenditure by monthly income per household and commodity category, industrial workers, Calcutta, 1958/59

Per household monthly income class (Rs) / Category	≤ 30	30 < 60	60 < 90	90 < 120	120 < 150	150 < 210	210 +	All [2]
Absolute amounts, in rupees								
Income	.	58.04	96.28	108.35	139.78	181.11	288.94	.
Saving and debt repayment	.	0.87	3.98	6.55	12.86	9.06	12.85	.
Consumption	69.72	57.17	88.70	101.80	126.92	172.05	276.09	105.79
Food	45.94	33.24	40.40	54.39	68.61	97.06	159.39	54.58
Cereals	22.60	9.78	14.29	20.75	24.56	40.85	67.62	20.36
Other food	23.34	23.46	26.11	33.64	44.05	56.21	91.77	34.22
Non-food [1]	23.78	23.93	48.30	47.41	58.31	74.99	116.70	51.21
of which: Remittances to dependants	—	6.70	22.29	15.16	14.62	13.51	7.88	17.07
Percentages of total income								
Income	.	100.00	100.00	100.00	100.00	100.00	100.00	.
Saving and debt repayment	.	1.50	4.29	6.05	9.20	5.00	4.45	.
Consumption	.	98.50	95.71	93.95	90.80	95.00	95.55	.
Food	.	57.27	43.59	50.20	49.08	53.59	55.16	
Cereals	.	16.85	15.42	19.15	17.57	22.56	23.40	.
Other food	.	40.42	28.17	31.05	31.51	31.04	31.76	.
Non-food [1]	.	41.23	52.11	43.75	41.72	41.41	40.39	.
of which: Remittances to dependants	.	11.54	23.15	13.99	10.46	7.46	2.73	.
Percentage distribution of families in sample	0.15	9.16	43.75	22.95	13.02	8.20	2.77	100.00

[1] Residual in table. Includes taxes, interest and litigation, and remittances to dependants. [2] Weighted average of entries in row.

Source: Government of India, Ministry of Labour and Employment, Labour Bureau: *Report on family living survey among industrial workers, 1958-59, Calcutta* (Simla, 1964), pp. 40, 41.

but for a smaller number of income classes than the total consumption table, the top monthly income class in the food table being Rs 100 and over. A direct comparison can be made, however, by separating total food consumption from the detailed food consumption table into cereals and other food, and combining the fifteen narrow income classes of the total consumption table into five broader ones (see table 58). Cereals consumption then clearly shows the behaviour of an "inferior good": per capita consumption shows absolute declines for per capita monthly incomes over Rs 100. Point to point cereals consumption elasticities calculated for the five income classes show a sharp fall from 0.4 for incomes around Rs 40 per month to 0.3 for incomes around Rs. 60 per month to -0.16 for incomes around Rs 95 per month. For the per capita monthly income class over Rs 100, the elasticity of cereals consumption is negative but close to zero.

The Hindustan Thompson 1969/70 survey shows a much lower share of total income going to remittances to dependants than does an earlier household expenditure study carried out by the Labour Bureau of the Government of India among Calcutta industrial workers in 1958/59.[1] Summary data from the Labour Bureau tabulations are given in table 59.

[1] Government of India, Ministry of Labour and Employment, Labour Bureau: *Report on family living survey among industrial workers, 1958-59, Calcutta*, op. cit.

Publications of the Government of India

Census of India
1961

    Volume I. *India.*
        Part II-A (i). *General population tables.*
        Part II-A (ii). *Union primary census abstracts.*
        Part II-B (ii). *General economic tables.*
        Part II-C (iii). *Migration tables.*
    Paper 1 of 1967. *Working force, 1901/1961.*
    Monograph Series. No. 2. *Calcutta—the primate city,* by A. Ghosh.

1971

    Series 1. *India.*
        Paper 1 of 1971. Supplement. *Provisional population totals.*
    Series 18. *West Bengal.*
        Paper 1 of 1971. *Provisional population totals.*

National Sample Survey

  8. *Report on preliminary survey of urban employment, September 1953.* New Delhi, Ministry of Finance, Department of of Economic Affairs, 1956.

 17. *Report on sample survey of employment in Calcutta, 1953.* With a foreword by P. C. Mahalanobis. Delhi, Cabinet Secretariat, 1959.

 34. *Tables with notes on employment and unemployment, Tenth Round: December 1955-May 1956.* Delhi, Cabinet Secretariat, 1960.

 52. *Tables with notes on employment and unemployment, Eleventh and Twelfth Rounds: August 1956-August 1957.* Delhi, Cabinet Secretariat, 1961.

 53. *Tables with notes on internal migration, Ninth, Eleventh, Twelfth and Thirteenth Rounds: May 1955-May 1958.* Delhi, Cabinet Secretariat, 1962.

 62. *Report on employment and unemployment, Ninth Round: Supplementary to Report No. 16: May-November 1955.* Delhi, Cabinet Secretariat, 1962.

 63. *Tables with notes on employment and unemployment in urban areas, Thirteenth Round: September 1957-May 1958.* Delhi, Cabinet Secretariat, 1962.

85. *Tables with notes on employment and unemployment in urban areas, Fourteenth Round: July 1958-June 1959.* Delhi, Cabinet Secretariat, 1964.

103. *Tables with notes on urban labour force, Sixteenth Round: July 1960-June 1961.* Delhi, Cabinet Secretariat, 1966.

126. *Tables with notes on internal migration, Fourteenth Round: July 1958-June 1959, Fifteenth Round: July 1959-June 1960.* Delhi, Cabinet Secretariat, 1968.

127. *Tables with notes on urban labour force, Seventeenth Round: September 1961-July 1962.* Delhi, Cabinet Secretariat, 1969.

152. *Tables with notes on urban labour force, Eighteenth Round: February 1963-January 1964.* Delhi, Cabinet Secretariat, 1969.

157. *Tables with notes on urban employment and unemployment, Fifteenth Round: July 1959-June 1960.* Delhi, Cabinet Secretariat, 1969.

163. *Tables with notes on urban labour force, Nineteenth Round: July 1964-June 1965.* Delhi, Cabinet Secretariat, 1970.

166. *Tables with notes on urban labour force, Twentieth Round: July 1965-June 1966.* Delhi, Cabinet Secretariat, 1970.

181. *Tables with notes on urban labour force, Twenty-first Round: July 1966-June 1967.* Delhi, Cabinet Secretariat, 1971.

*Other publications
of the Government of India.*

Economic survey, 1971-72. New Delhi, 1972.

Location of industry in India. New Delhi, 1945.

Cabinet Secretariat, Department of Statistics, Central Statistical Organisation. *Statistical abstract, India* (entitled *Statistical abstract of the Indian Union* from 1958 to 1967 inclusive). New Series. Nos. 2 *(1950)* to 16 *(1968)*.

— — — Industrial Statistics Wing. *Annual survey of industries, 1959.*

— — — — *Annual survey of industries, 1966, census sector (provisional results), general review.* Calcutta, 1969.

— — — — *Annual survey of industries, 1967, census sector (provisional results), general review.* Calcutta, 1970; also detailed mimeographed version, 1972.

Ministry of Labour and Employment, Labour Bureau. *Report on family living survey among industrial workers, 1958-59, Calcutta.* Simla, 1964.

Ministry of Works, Housing and Urban Development, Town and Country Planning Organisation, Joint Planning Board for South East Resource Region. *Regional development plan for South East Resource Region: Summary report.* New Delhi, 1972, mimeographed.

Planning Commission. *Report of the committee of experts on unemployment estimates.* New Delhi, 1970.

— Perspective Planning Division. *Draft Fourth Plan: Material and financial balances, 1964-65, 1970-71 and 1975-76.* New Delhi, 1966.

Publications of the Government of West Bengal

Economic review, year 1970-71. Calcutta, 1971.

Economic review, year 1971-72. Calcutta, 1972.

Bureau of Applied Economics and Statistics. *A preliminary report on unemployment survey, 1971, in West Bengal.* Calcutta, 1972.

— *Statistical handbook, 1970.* Calcutta, 1971.

Calcutta Metropolitan Development Authority (CMDA). *1971-1972 plan programme, Expenditure progress as on 31 December 1971, Statement No. 6, Effective date 17 January 1972.* Calcutta, mimeographed.

Development and Planning (Town and Country Planning) Department, Calcutta Metropolitan Planning Organisation (CMPO). *A memorandum on a perspective plan for Calcutta Metropolitan District and West Bengal, 1971-1989.* Calcutta, 1971.

— *A note on the economic development programme for the Calcutta Metropolitan District.* A draft for discussion. Calcutta 1972, mimeographed.

— *A note on the estimation of employment potential during the Fourth Five-Year Plan period based on CMD development schemes.* Calcutta, 1971, typescript.

— *Basic development plan for the Calcutta Metropolitan District, 1966-1986.* Calcutta, 1966.

— *Bustee improvement programme: Calcutta and Howrah.* Calcutta, 1964, revised 1967.

— *Interim report: Housing, Calcutta Metropolitan District.* Calcutta, 1967.

— *The socio-economic plan frame,* by H. Banerji. Calcutta, 1966, mimeographed.

— *Traffic and transportation plan for the Calcutta Metropolitan District, 1966-1986.* Calcutta, 1967.

— Industrial Planning Team. *Report on the engineering industry, West Bengal, 1951-1968.* Calcutta, 1968.

— Traffic and Transportation Division. *Traffic study for the proposed rapid transit system and suburban dispersal line in Calcutta.* Calcutta, 1971.

Labour Directorate, Statistics, Research and Publication Branch. *Labour in West Bengal, 1970.* Calcutta, 1971.

— — *Labour in West Bengal, 1971.* Calcutta, 1972.

— Statistics Branch. *Handbook of labour statistics, West Bengal, 1970.* Calcutta, 1971.

Metropolitan Transport Project (Railways). *Calcutta mass transit study, 1970-1971 : Dum Dum to Tollyganj.* Calcutta, 1971.

State Planning Board. *Comprehensive area development programme (CADP): A new strategy for development.* Calcutta, 1973.

— *West Bengal's approach to the Fifth Five-Year Plan, 1974-1979.* Calcutta, 1972.

State Statistical Bureau. *Rehabilitation of refugees: A statistical survey, 1955.* Calcutta, 1956.

— *Report of the sample survey for estimating the socio-economic characteristics of displaced persons migrating from Eastern Pakistan to the State of West Bengal.* Calcutta, 1951.

— *Report on the survey of unemployment in Calcutta and Calcutta industrial areas, 1959.* Calcutta, 1966.

— *Statistical handbook, 1966.* Calcutta, 1967.

Other publications

Bairoch, Paul. *Urban unemployment in developing countries: The nature of the problem and proposals for its solution.* Geneva, ILO, 1973.

Bandyopadhyay, D., Labour Commissioner, West Bengal. *The rate of wages of agricultural workers: A case study of two Bankura villages.* Calcutta, 1972.

Bhatia, V. G. "Employment potential of roads". In Ronald G. Ridker and Harold Lubell (ed.): *Employment and unemployment problems of the Near East and South Asia* (Delhi, Vikas, 1971), Vol. II, pp. 765-770.

Bengal Chamber of Commerce and Industry. *West Bengal,* An analytical study. New Delhi, Bombay and Calcutta, Oxford and IBH Publishing Co., 1971.

Bose, A. N. "Continuing semi-colonial character—The basic problem of the Indian metropolis". In *Indian Journal of Regional Science*, Vol. III, No. 1, 1971.

Bose, Ashish. "The urbanisation process in South and Southeast Asia". In Leo Jakobson and Ved Prakash (ed.): *Urbanisation and national development* (Beverly Hills, Sage Publications, 1971).

Bose, Nirmal Kumar. *Calcutta, 1964: A social survey.* Bombay, Lalvani, 1968.

"Calcutta and the World Bank Mission". In *Economic Weekly* (Bombay), Vol. XII, No. 40, 1 October 1960.

Chatterjee, A. B. *Howrah: A study of social geography.* Calcutta, U. Chatterjee, 1967.

Chakraverti, N. C. *Report on the survey of refugee population in West Bengal (1948).* Calcutta, 1949, mimeographed.

Chakraverty, K. R. *A study of the life-time in-migration to Calcutta city.* Ph.D. dissertation, University of Pennsylvania, Department of Demography, 1967, typescript.

Chalmers Wright, F. *Licensed delegation of company management in India, with special reference to the "managing agency" system.* Calcutta, Bengal Chamber of Commerce and Industry, 1959.

Franda, Marcus F. *Radical politics in West Bengal.* Cambridge, Mass., and London, Massachusetts Institute of Technology Press, 1971.

Gait, E. A. "Population". In *The Imperial Gazetteer of India* (Oxford, Clarendon Press, 1909), Vol. I.

Hindustan Thompson Associates Ltd. *A study of food habits in Calcutta.* Calcutta, Hindustan Thompson Associates Ltd. on behalf of United States Agency for International Development, 1972.

India and Foreign Review (New Delhi), Vol. 9, No. 9, 15 February 1972.

Indian Chamber of Commerce. *Employment trends in West Bengal.* Background paper II, Seminar on growth of employment opportunities, Calcutta, Indian Chamber of Commerce, 5 May 1972.

International Labour Office. *Concepts of labour force utilisation.* Geneva, 1971.

— *Employment, incomes and equality: A strategy for increasing productive employment in Kenya,* Report of an inter-agency team financed by the United Nations Development Programme and organised by the International Labour Office. Geneva, 1972.

— *Matching employment opportunities and expectations: A programme of action for Ceylon,* The report of an inter-agency team organised by the International Labour Office. Geneva, 1971.

— "Measuring the adequacy of employment in developing countries". In *Journal of Development Planning* (New York, United Nations, Department of Economic and Social Affairs), 1972, No. 5, pp. 145-164.

Kingsley, G. Thomas, and Kristof, Frank S. *A housing policy for metropolitan Calcutta,* A recommendation to the Ford Foundation Advisory Planning Group with the Calcutta Metropolitan Planning Organisation. Calcutta, 1971.

Mitra, Asok. *Calcutta, India's city.* Calcutta, New Age, 1963.

Moorhouse, Geoffrey. *Calcutta.* London, Weidenfeld and Nicholson, 1971.

Mouly, Jean. "Some remarks on the concepts of employment, underemployment and unemployment". In *International Labour Review* (Geneva, ILO), Vol. 105, No. 2, February 1972, pp. 155-610.

National Council for Applied Economic Research: *Nature of educated unemployment in urban areas.* New Delhi, forthcoming.

Pakrasi, Kanti B. *The uprooted: A sociological study of the refugees of West Bengal, India.* Calcutta, Editions Indian, 1971.

Piplai, Tapan, and Majumdar, Niloy. "Internal migration in India: Some socio-economic implications". In *Sankhyā: The Indian Journal of Statistics* (Calcutta), Series B, Vol. 31, Parts 3 and 4, December 1969, pp. 518-519.

Reserve Bank of India. *Survey of small engineering units in Howrah*, Report of a survey undertaken by Jadavpur University. Calcutta and Bombay, 1964.

Sen, Sanjoy. Welcome address, Seminar on growth of employment opportunities, Calcutta, Indian Chamber of Commerce, 5 May 1972.

Sen, S. N. *The city of Calcutta: A socio-economic survey, 1954-55 to 1957-58*. Calcutta, Bookland, 1960.

— and Piplai, Tapan. *Industrial relations in the jute industry in West Bengal*, A case study. Calcutta, Bookland, 1968.

Sethuraman, S. V. "Prospects for increasing employment in the Indian manufacturing sector". In Ronald G. Ridker and Harold Lubell (ed.): *Employment and unemployment problems of the Near East and South Asia* (Delhi, Vikas, 1971), Vol. II, pp. 587-638.

United Nations. *Demographic yearbook, 1971*—23rd Issue, Special topic: *Population census statistics I* (New York, 1972).

United Nations Educational, Scientific and Cultural Organisation (UNESCO), Research Centre on Social and Economic Development in Southern Asia. *Social aspects of small industries in India: Studies in Howrah and Bombay of selected turning shops, blacksmithies and art silk units.* Delhi, 1962.

United Nations Industrial Development Organisation. *Construction industry.* UNIDO Monographs on Industrial Development, No. 2. New York, United Nations, 1969; Sales No. E. 69. II. B. 39, Vol. 2.

Visaria, Pravin. "The provisional 1971 census data on the size and composition of the working force". In *Times of India*, 9 July 1971.

The three maps appended to this study are published solely to make it easier to understand: an endeavour has been made to ensure that every place and geographical entity mentioned in the text can either be found on at least one of the three maps, or can be roughly located on the basis of footnotes referring to places that are themselves to be found on the maps.

Map 1 is based, by permission of the Calcutta Metropolitan Planning Organisation, on the map facing page 6 of the *Basic Development Plan, Calcutta Metropolitan District, 1966-1986*. Maps 2 and 3 are based, again by permission, on maps of the International Bank for Reconstruction and Development, with a number of modifications (mainly additions) to meet the needs of readers of the present study. The boundaries shown and the designations used do not imply endorsement or acceptance by the Bank or the International Labour Office.